Radical   Rational   Space   Time

Idea Networks in Photography

Paul Berger

Leroy Searle

Douglas Wadden

Henry Art Gallery

University of Washington, Seattle

This book has been prepared in conjunction
with an exhibition of the same name exhibited
at the Henry Art Gallery, University of
Washington, Seattle, March 11-May 15, 1983.
This book has been funded by the Henry
Gallery Association.

ISBN: 0-935558-10-1
Library of Congress Catalog Card Number: 83-080314

Edited by Joseph N. Newland.
Designed by Douglas Wadden.

Type set in Helvetica by Paul O. Giesey/Adcrafters,
Portland, Oregon.
Scan and camera duotones and lithography by
Graphic Arts Center, Portland, Oregon.
Printed on 80 lb. Vintage Velvet book and a
laminated 12 pt. Kromekote cover.
Binding by Lincoln & Allen, Portland, Oregon.

Foreword

One of the unique aspects of this book and its companion exhibition for me has been my privilege to observe the collaboration between Paul Berger, photographer and teacher, Douglas Wadden, designer and teacher, Leroy Searle, author and teacher, and Joseph Newland, art publication editor.

In 1981, Paul Berger, Associate Professor of Photography at the University of Washington, was invited by the Gallery to curate the exhibition that shaped the content of this publication, and, at the same time, Douglas Wadden, Associate Professor of Design, was asked to design a companion book. From the beginning it was our collective intent that the exhibition and book would become two different but interdependent statements about photographers who use doubles, sequences, grids, overlays and other types of arrays to express their ideas. Paul Berger framed the definitions, chose the photographers, made the final image selection and collaborated on the installation of the exhibition. Using the same material, Douglas Wadden acted as author of a visual text and orchestrated the publication—a second view of *Radical Rational/Space Time.* Leroy Searle, an Associate Professor of English who has written on photographic discourse and culture and photography, wrote an overview of the issues and connecting text relating to each of the photographers. Joseph Newland, the Gallery's editor of publications, has once again skillfully crafted an art publication, as he has done many times for the Gallery. In addition to their professionalism, each person brought to the collaborative meetings a mutual belief, enthusiasm and respect for each other's ability to understand and interpret the issues being presented.

One of the Henry Art Gallery's basic functions is to be an intellectual forum within the University and region for such a visual and verbal dialogue. This project has given the Gallery, because of the talents of those involved, the opportunity to explore complicated nuances of photographic time and space.

Moreover, this project is timely and significant for the University because of the developing photography program in the School of Art. For the past ten years, the faculty have worked diligently to expand the photographic community in Seattle and especially to strengthen the University's program. *Radical Rational/Space Time: Idea Networks in Photography* is an indication to the public of their success as teachers, artists, curators and authors.

It gives me great pleasure to express my appreciation, in addition to the "gang of four," to every one of the Gallery staff who have added importantly to the project's planning and presentation, and especially to Chris Bruce for a brilliant installation. Our gratitude goes to the Henry Gallery Association for their intellectual and financial support of the book and the exhibition. The Association is the backbone of the Gallery's programming efforts, and any success we enjoy is directly related to their efforts and generosity. The trustees have time and time again responded with great enthusiasm and dedication to a variety of needs. Mrs. William W. Hoppin, Jr., President, and the Association's Director, Mrs. John E. Z. Caner, have played major roles in bringing this project to fruition. To them and the trustees goes a special thank you. Last, but not least, a heartfelt expression of gratitude is due to the photographers who have shared their superb creative eyes and minds with us. The project started as an idea, but in the final analysis it is their photography that is being celebrated.

Harvey West
Director
Henry Art Gallery

This publication emerged as a documentation of shared ideas as well as of the work of several photographers.

Some three years ago I approached Harvey West with the suggestion that we had an unusual combination of resources available to present an innovative exhibit and catalogue dealing with contemporary issues in photography. He, my colleague Paul Berger and I wished to undertake a very deliberate exploration of specific photographic relationships, particularly questions of space, time and various methods of array. Of equal importance was the unique potential for critical elaboration that exists between photographic images and their reproduction in book form. Because of the very nature of the photographic issues concerned, juxtaposition, sequencing and page structure can amplify and extend these ideas beyond the apparent independence of individual images. The deceptive simplicity of many of these photographs is intentionally and justifiably compounded by the expanding conceptual network of visual/verbal organization and discourse.

In his role as guest curator for the Henry Art Gallery, Paul began the project by selecting artists to be included in the exhibition. His final definitions of the issues and inclusions were based on previous discussions with Leroy Searle and Rod Slemmons, who is now Associate Curator of Photography at the Seattle Art Museum. Leroy joined in the project especially for the publication and performed the essential interactive role of writing specifically for this layout. The concept, image selection and design of the book reflect my interpretation of the ideas. Joseph Newland and I collaborated on the final infrastructure of the publication. Joseph, Leroy, Paul and I have extended an interactive attitude to our own methods of organization, sharing in each others' decisions and rearranging the traditional sequence of events by which most publications of this kind are generated.

The deliberate exploration that I referred to earlier is central to the order of the book, which abandons the typical alphabetically or chronologically sequenced layout for one that allows the images to confront their conceptual counterparts in varying ways. Often the photographs attracted one another, revealing similar nuances of perspective, subject matter and treatment, comparisons that are uniquely possible in a book through modified scale, detailing and neutralization of tone. Structurally, the first section presents a visual summary of primary issues, for which Leroy Searle has provided an overview. The remaining pages are divided into two main categories of concern—pairs or doubles, for which Paul Berger has written an essay, and multiple arrays, for which Leroy Searle has continued the analysis.

In the book I have transposed, inverted, isolated and taken details of many of the photographs in an effort to expand the viewer's understanding of the ideas. This is done partly to "open up" seemingly fixed relationships inherent in a more rigid presentation, and, more importantly, to override any conclusions that might be based on an assumed logic or perceived reality which limit interpretation or even mislead. Where we felt it necessary to identify our deviation from the "norm," we have provided brief analytical statements to explain the intention of the layout and the source of the detail or picture portion shown. I hope that the structure we have created is an appropriately simple and sympathetic realization of our intentions.

I am exceedingly grateful to the Henry Art Gallery for the opportunity to compile this material and bring a collaborative group of very different professionals together to share their interests and expertise. Also, I wish to extend my special thanks to Graphic Arts Center, Portland, Oregon, for the excellence of their contribution to all aspects of the production of this publication.

Douglas Wadden

Unless noted otherwise, photographs are a single negative printed on a single sheet. Dates given are those of the negatives. Full information on each work can be found in the checklist of the exhibition that begins on page 68.

Eadweard Muybridge

Abe Edgington Trotting, from *The Horse in
Motion,* 1878
Print made from 12 negatives
Collection of R. Joseph and Elaine R. Monsen

Marion Faller and Hollis Frampton

Sunflower reclining (var. "Mammoth Russian"),
Number 39, "Sixteen Studies from *Vegetable
Locomotion,"* 1975
Print made from 12 negatives
Courtesy of the artists and Visual Studies
Workshop Gallery, Rochester

With *The Horse in Motion,* Eadweard Muybridge began a large, sometimes sprawling project in the history of photography. I refer not only to his monumental work, *Animal Locomotion,* in which he documented a bewildering variety of animals doing an equally bewildering variety of things, but also to a collective project, in which a great many other photographers, thinkers, and writers have played a part.[1] When we look at the now famous display, *Abe Edgington Trotting,* we are likely to think of the controversy (even if it did not happen) over whether or not a trotting horse ever has all four legs off the ground at the same time.

Clearly, he does.[2]

But if we look closely at this work, presented in a matrix to be viewed from left to right and top to bottom, we will see the grounds for another kind of controversy that did not happen: in this case, it is hard to formulate a question over which to disagree. This work is called, *"The Horse in Motion,* Illustrated by Muybridge." "Illustrated"? What illustrates what here? The "illustration" is the work itself; and if it is not, then it "illustrates" an event (the horse trotting past Muybridge's patented apparatus) that has nothing directly to do with Muybridge.

This is outrageous.

Perhaps we should pity the poor writer of the caption, confronted with this work, made by a patented apparatus. He had only a set of conventions to work with, conventions which led one to think that an "illustration" was ancilliary to an event, a story, a text, while "illustrating" was the work done by an individual artist. How could he even think that an "illustration" itself could BE a text, a story, and an event, all at the same time—while WORDS are relegated to the subordinate, ancilliary position meant for the "illustration?"

What IS "illustration" anyway?

In *Prints and Visual Communication,* William Ivins describes the tradition through which this problem has been defined. While Ivins notes that it is in part a "tradition of snobbery"[3] where photography is concerned, it is primarily a tradition of worked artifacts— pictures, that is, made by hand and produced through a step-by-step process.

The set of conventions and principles by which prints were made, passed on from master to apprentice, Ivins calls the "syntax" of picture making. In this sense of the term, Ivins notes, photographs are images without syntax,[4] sharing with other prints a pictorial format, but using radically different processes of image production.

What is important in this observation, however, is that the "syntax" employed to assemble graphic parts into a pictorial whole not only constructs pictures, but pictures with meanings. The difficulty is that another kind of "syntax" is implied in interpreting meaning that may not correspond directly with the "syntax" of picture production.

When we look at *The Horse in Motion*, for example, we read the pictures as a text, line by line, as a narrative progression in which meaning is determined by the correspondence of sequential frames in the display with temporal segments of the horse's movement through space.

In this way, we rely on the conventions and syntax of writing to read such photographs as if they were transparent and merely told us something about horses; but for Muybridge (as for later photographers), the vitality of these photographs lies in what they tell us about the way we see, think, and represent things to ourselves. The controversy about galloping horses, for example, had almost nothing to do with horses: it was, rather, a realization that the way artists had long depicted galloping horses was "incorrect," in the sense that it did not correspond to the action itself. Thus, the controversy was itself enveloped in the world of "art"—despite the obvious fact that *Animal Locomotion* was also a work of "science."

"Science"?

While Muybridge intended his work to aid artists in their depiction of motion, eighteen drawings copied from Muybridge's photographs were published in *Scientific American* in October 1878,[5] and the controversy aroused by these photographs was owing primarily to the fact that they showed surprising and unexpected aspects of familiar events. Thus, it hardly makes sense to say of these photographs that they belong to the domain of "art" or "science" when they so clearly mark a shared boundary, or an overlapping region within a circle of confusion. They belong, that is, in the space of inquiry, where activity is carried out in the service of knowledge and understanding.

When Muybridge showed how to stop time in order to reveal unknown aspects of motion, the result was a radical concept of time as a spatial image. Time, that is, appears only as a sequence of moments, each one bearing a distinct image identity. So too, the simple logic of the grid—both as the background to measure the progress of the horse, and the whole array of individual images—takes this radical idea of time as the principle on which to rationalize space. It makes of space not an endless expanse, but a delimited field, with a simple, abstract syntax. In that field, the role of the image is entirely relational. It relates the known to the unknown, time to space, image to image, action to action, in a radical, rational matrix.

Notes for this essay will be found on page 11.

When we then consider such works by Marion Faller and Hollis Frampton as *Sunflower Reclining,* from their series, *Vegetable Locomotion*, we can laugh heartily at the witty inversion of Muybridge: we know that the giant sunflower, cut down, will only fall, from left to right, at the exponential rate of gravity. There will be no unexpected discovery, no surprise. But like all true wit, it allows us a discovery of another sort: we are made conscious that time is radical and space rational only by how we picture it to ourselves. We can just as well make pure space radical—the blank, empty grid without event in which time appears not as the frozen image, but a ratio among images as states of space. In this case, the root or "radical" of time is not the single image, but instead the mental expectation of change.

These are simple ideas.

That does not make them easy. The work presented in this book is a carefully collected sample of the historical project that Muybridge, perhaps inadvertently, began. From simple ideas of illustration, picture, time, and space, articulated according to equally simple strategies of display, there appears a network of ideas, a rich and variable system of inquiry, a way of making pictures that are copiously meaningful. The matrix employed by Muybridge and adapted by others for different purposes figures prominently in this work, not because it is intrinsically significant, but because it insists that we see images in networks, according to relations, and not just as isolated, sumptuous artifacts.

Thus, when photographers begin to conceive their art as the making of visual networks, constellations, sequences, etc., they move from a conception of "art" narrowly defined by aesthetic concerns to a conception of "art" as a form of investigation and a form of cultural communication. In this broader conception, familiar distinctions—as between "art" and "science"—cease to be sharp; and art itself becomes a science-like activity, an orderly inquiry that requires imagination and discipline in equal portions. The work produced under such a conception lies primarily in the deployment of ideas in networks, where meaning is produced by interactions among images, in the context of expectations entertained by viewers.

This book starts with pictures, juxtaposed across two pages; it is meant to be an idea network itself. Two works, separated by a century, communicate by their common participation in a strategy, just as they differ dialectically. In the images, that is, are contained complex relations that unfold over time, through a process of controversy, assimilation, and transformation. I have already hinted at one such transformation, in the inversion of priorities between words and pictures: in this book, the argument is carried in the images; and the book has been conceived and assembled in a collaborative effort devoted to as rich and comprehensive an examination of visual discourse as we could provide in short compass.

As the analytical and descriptive captions indicate, we have taken some liberties with these photographs, entirely justified, we believe, by the manifest visual intelligence of the photographs themselves. These are acutely conscious and deliberate artifacts. They set about to discover features of our common lives with the direct compassion of all art, but with the rigor of philosophy, concerned to understand the grounds on which our common lives are possible. What these works have in common is the implicit confidence that we can make experience intelligible in visual terms, but that doing so requires an experimental attitude and speculative discipline.

The range of the work is exceptionally broad. Ellen Manchester, Mark Klett, JoAnn Verburg and others who participated in the Rephotographic Survey Project (RSP) set about the gigantic task of repeating photographs taken in the great Surveys of the West in the last century, by locating the exact position of the earlier photographers and making an exposure under virtually identical photographic conditions. As Paul Berger recounts in his essay later in this book, these photographs, separated by a century, transform (and radically complicate) our notions of time, just as other photographic "doubles" transform our understanding of how space and time interact to form the world we inhabit.

Bill Ganzel, in a related but very different project involving rephotographing the subjects of well known Farm Security Administration (FSA) photographs from the Depression, produces photographic doubles as cultural documents, accompanied by oral accounts by the subjects. In these works, we see the compression of cultural time by the juxtaposition of images that share a subject, but differ radically in meaning. Those famous photographs of the Depression, by Lange and Rothstein and others, have become monuments in our collective memories, so that the persons in them, photographed today, appear also in the idea network of another time, our own time. Repetition, in this case, preserves only the identity of persons, and thereby increases our awareness of change in our cultural milieu.

While Ganzel thus records the complex drama of cultural change, Frank Gohlke's *Aftermath* series shows us an equally complex drama of physical change—which, ironically, turns out to be a trenchant commentary on contemporary culture. In recording the damage of the Wichita Falls tornado, and then returning one year later to photograph the same locations, Gohlke provides an ironic demonstration that nature and man both alter space, the first, without apparent design, and the second, apparently without design. Thus it appears that what we know of a space is just what we do to it; and Wichita Falls, in these juxtaposed photographs becomes a metaphor of devastation. In a place where tornados recur (this disaster is not unique), these photographs show both the indiscriminate violence of nature, and the doggedness of people who resist it.

Joseph Deal

San Fernando, California, 1979, from *The Fault Zone,* 1981
Seattle Art Museum

These are just examples of the way in which photographic display has become a syntax and a form of visual logic. Grids, sequences, and other strategies may be viewed as somewhat arbitrary conveniences; but once employed, such strategies mark the beginning of an inquiry, the unfolding of a system of visual and cultural discourse that is as various as it is simple.

In reading this book, there is not one "story" but a multiplicity of messages, all based on the same general idea. It is, as Immanuel Kant argued in *The Critique of Pure Reason,* that what we know directly depends on the manifold of time and space.[6] But unlike Kant, the photographers represented in this book do not presume that this "manifold" is determined only in concepts or according to categories, which, like general nouns or verbs, give an abstract identity to all we can know. On the contrary, these photographers show the incessant breaking of categories as they trace, instead, imaginative and image-based relations that prevent us from subsuming particulars under a general rule, but require us to preserve variations and subtle differences in our generalizations.

In the work of Bernd and Hilla Becher, or Gary Metz, for example, repetitive photographs of objects belonging to a single category show us how we can generalize without reductiveness, and how we can form ideas without becoming entangled in metaphysical puzzles about whether universals exist.

In the manifestly more intricate work of Joseph Deal, William S. Paris, and Robbert Flick, on the other hand, we find explorations of visual entanglements and implications that play directly on our conceptual habits and assumptions. These are photographers who appear only too glad to accept whatever is there to be photographed, in the knowledge that what one can see and what one can think about it are not perfectly symmetrical.

What "exists" is no problem here: how we make sense of it is. These photographers demonstrate in diverse ways that in repetition we discover principles of identity; and in redundancy we discover principles of

substitution. In visual terms, the syntax of the photographic matrix or array produces order and meaning as the product of identity and substitution: the individual photograph identifies a single state of the space/time manifold, while the display fixes it in a network of relations. Then, by repeating the same ordering operation—as, for example, constructing a grid, or assembling a sequence—one substitutes new images, new identities, in an evolving constellation of visual consciousness, that may span a century (as in the work of the RSP) or a few moments (as in the work of Eve Sonneman); and may be as abstract as mathematical propositions (as in the work of William Paris) or as moving and intimate as a familial elegy as in Esther Parada's *Memory Warp* series.

Just as these photographers take the world we inhabit as their domain of investigation, so we have taken these photographs as the constellated domain of this book. By repetition and redundancy, identity and substitution, we have devised this network of ideas as a sample and a model of the larger network which photographers today are exploring.

L.S.

above
William Henry Jackson

Montezuma's Cathedral, Garden of the Gods.
1873
United States Geological Survey, Denver

below
Mark Klett and JoAnn Verburg
for the Rephotographic Survey Project

Faulted Rocks, Garden of the Gods, Colorado.
1977
Courtesy of the artists

Mark Klett and JoAnn Verburg
for the Rephotographic Survey Project

Faulted Rocks, Garden of the Gods, Colorado.
1977

Arthur Rothstein

Fleeing a Dust Storm [from left, Milton, Arthur, and Darrell Coble].
Cimarron County, Oklahoma
April 1936
Library of Congress, Washington, D.C.

1. Work represented here is closely related to other photographic strategies, especially in sequential photography. For further discussion (and bibliographic matter), see Ann Wilkes Tucker, ed., *Target III: In Sequence. Photographic Sequences from The Target Collection of American Photography* (Houston: The Museum of Fine Arts, 1982).

2. To be more precise, the controversy was much more pronounced on the movement of galloping horses, where people were surprised (and incredulous) to find that the horse has all four legs off the ground only when they are tucked under the midsection. See Beaumont Newall, *The History of Photography* 4th ed. (New York: The Museum of Modern Art, 1978), pp. 83-89.

3. William M. Ivins, Jr., *Prints and Visual Communication* (1953; rpt. Cambridge, MA: MIT Press, 1969), p. 116.

4. Ivins, pp. 60-61; 128-129.

5. See Newhall, p. 84.

6. Immanuel Kant, *The Critique of Pure Reason*, trans. Norman Kemp Smith (New York: St. Martin's Press, 1964), esp. Introduction.

"All the days was about alike then. For a three-year-old kid, you just go outside and play, dust blows and sand blows, and you don't know any difference. One evening, a black duster come in here from the north. We had kerosene lamps. And it got so dark you couldn't see with kerosene lamps.

"Last spring we had some pretty bad days. They weren't the old black dusters, but I mean, there was plenty of dust in the air.

"I don't really know why I like living here. I guess just 'cause this country's home. Dad always said that if anybody ever come here and wear out two pairs of shoes here, they'd never leave. Back in the thirties, my dad had some relatives in California that was fairly wealthy, an aunt and uncle, and they wanted him to get outa here. They said they'd pay his way out to California, the whole family, but he said he wouldn't go. He was just a hard-headed Coble, I guess. He was pretty independent. I just imagine he thought that if it was going to be somebody else's money, why, he wasn't gonna go, period."

Darrel Coble

Bill Ganzel

13

Darrel Coble in his home. *On the wall is a painting by a local woman copied from Rothstein's photograph. In 1977, Darrel lived about 12 miles from where the photograph was taken. Arthur, his father, and Milton, his older brother, had died, and Darrel died in 1980.*

Cimarron County, Oklahoma
September 1977
Courtesy of the artist

Frank Gohlke

Southwest Parkway near Fairway, looking west,
April 15, 1979, from *Aftermath: The Wichita Falls*
Tornado, 1982
Courtesy of the artist

***Southwest Parkway near Fairway, looking west,
June 1980,*** from *Aftermath: The Wichita Falls
Tornado,* 1982
Courtesy of the artist

Gary Metz

Two prints from the series *Hair Piece ("Every Force Has Its Form"–Shaker Saying).* 1977-1979
Courtesy of the artist

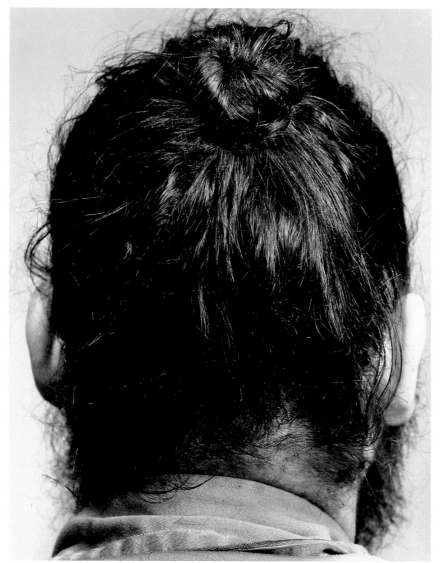 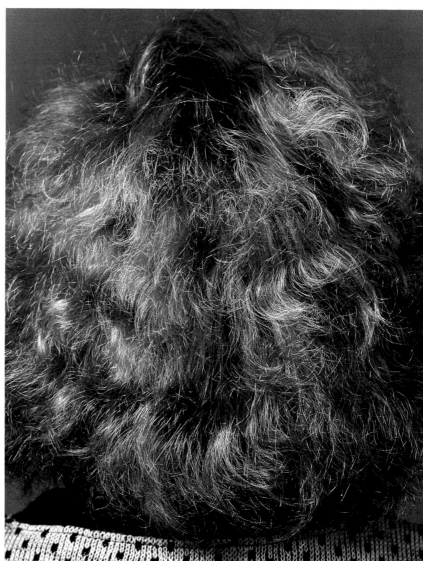

Bernd and Hilla Becher

Winding Towers. 1982
15 prints, mounted separately and displayed in
three rows of five
Courtesy of the artists and Sonnabend Gallery,
New York

Robbert Flick

Solstice Canyon #8. 1982
Prints made from 81 negatives in nine rows of nine
Courtesy of the artist and Tortue Gallery, Santa
Monica

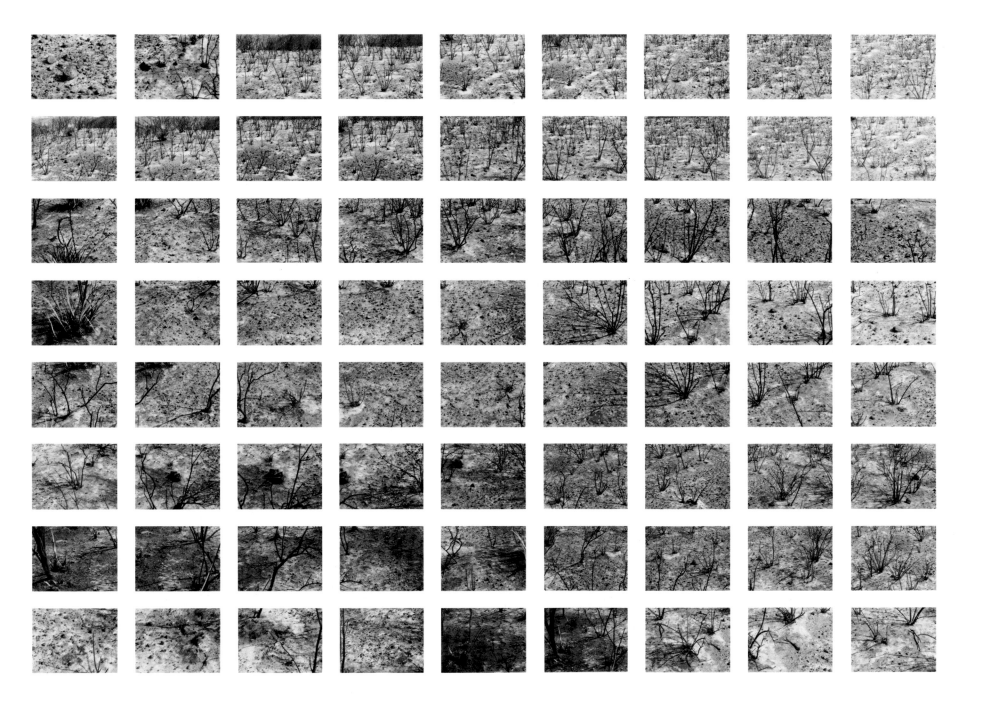

San Bernardino, California, 1978 (I), from *The Fault Zone,* 1981
Seattle Art Museum

above
Timothy H. O'Sullivan

Spanish Inscriptions, Inscription Rock. 1873
United States Geological Survey, Denver

below
Rick Dingus
for the Rephotographic Survey Project

Inscriptions #20 on the walking tour, Inscription Rock, New Mexico. 1978
Courtesy of the artist

This RSP pair marks a significant departure from most other pairs. Here, an "alternate view" acknowledges the limits of strict vantage point replication to record cultural transformations. Inscription Rock, denuded of 20th-century graffiti, is here seen as number 20 on a Park Service walking tour.

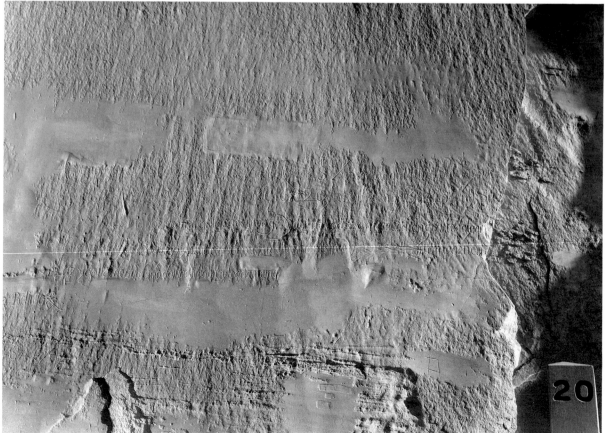

Doubling: This then That

"While only a select few can appreciate the discoveries of the geologists or the exact measurements of the topographers, everyone can understand a picture."

New York Times, April 27, 1875

"Bring me men to match my mountains..."

Sam Walter Foss, "The Coming American," c. 1895[1]

Everyone looking at W. H. Jackson's photograph *Mountain of the Holy Cross* in 1875 understood that they were looking at a mountain in the far off Rockies; this was fact. The Holy Cross, however, was from their own pictorial backyard, and its transcendent location both "out there" and "back here" was the basis for a different but simultaneous kind of "understanding." Photographers such as W. H. Jackson were only one component of the United States Geological Survey teams sent by the federal government in the 1870s to chart vast areas of the American West. Record-breaking measurements were expected from *all* members of the vanguard Survey teams sent out to explore and accurately describe that majestic territory, but the power and popularity of the resulting photographs took the measure of something else. It was more than specific physical properties that the team was expected to relay, and viewers in the 1870s were more than ready to see photographic reports of the unknown and rugged Far West in the larger cultural context of Romance and Manifest Destiny.

The way we understand photographs, then or now, may seem automatic, but it is certainly not simple. This phenomenon was described quite elegantly by the photographer Brassai in 1968: "The photograph has a double destiny....It is the daughter of the world of externals, of the living second, and as such will always keep something of the historic or scientific document about it; but it is also the daughter of the rectangle, a child of the beaux-arts..."[2]

This duality is fundamental to our understanding of photography. As an image, the photograph can be both document and picture, artifact and art, visual map and carrier of cultural meaning. Although some photographers may place their concern at one extreme or the other, all photographs are necessarily situated somewhere along the continuum between the two poles. But where a viewer "locates" any particular photograph along this continuum, i.e., how they understand it, is determined by more than just the photograph itself. The way we understand a photograph, despite the *New York Times'* claim of 1875, is a complex and rapid negotiation between the photograph as both physical fact and cultural image. Since we commonly speak of a photograph as being "taken" from the flux and flow of space through time, our attempt to understand it is our natural urge to place the image back into a context of our own making, on our own terms. But this context is never confined, despite titles such as *Mountain of the Holy Cross,* to simple time/space coordinates. We place the image in a cultural time as well as a physical place, for our eyes and minds don't see photographs the way cameras and lenses make them.

Although this placement process is operative whenever we look at *any* photograph, this essay will be concerned with a group of photographers who use a very specific strategy to examine the subtleties and complications of how such negotiation takes place. The strategy involves "doubles," two photographs presented as one image. These photographic pairs are images of the same place, person, or event, taken at two different times, anywhere from 100 years to seconds apart. By holding one factor constant—the place, person, or event— these doubles direct our attention towards the time that separates them. But as we shall see, our sense of time in a photograph is itself a complex duality of quantitative fact and acculturated sensibility.

The photographs of the Western Surveys are case studies of Brassai's observation: at the time they were taken, they served as visual, quantifiable facts, *and* conveyed in a more general way a sense of grandeur, beauty, and cultural sovereignty over that uncharted area. By having its picture taken, this "virgin" land was now both mapped and made landscape, relieved of the lack of identity that undoubtedly dominates whatever mountains do without men around them. Our appreciation of the Western Survey photographs has evolved as time passes, photographs multiply, and Destiny is Manifested, but because of the very nature of photographic veracity, the measurements, the "facts" reported through the camera lens 100 years ago, are unchanged. In this narrow aspect, these photographs are more than artistic impressions or responses to the Far West, as a painting, sketch, or poem might be; they are repeatable, spatial "scans"— a mechanically exact transposition of three-dimensional space onto a two-dimensional picture plane.

Although we can't repeat the past, or even agree on its history, we *can* repeat how a lens described a discrete space by simply returning there. This form of repetition is the basis for the work of the Rephotographic Survey Project, founded by Ellen Manchester, Mark Klett and JoAnn Verburg in 1976. The RSP began by developing a methodology of "rephotography," i.e., establishing working procedures for duplicating camera lens position, as well as the time of day and year of the original 19th-century photograph. Initially, the source of replication was W. H. Jackson's photographic work with Hayden's (later the U.S.G.S.), Survey in Colorado, 1873. The project was subsequently expanded to include neighboring Western states, and the work of other 19th-century Survey photographers, notably A. J. Russell and T. H. O'Sullivan. In the final display, the original Survey photograph (or a copy print) is placed next to a same size "rephotograph." Since the vantage point, the point in space from which the original Survey photographer chose to make his picture, was virtually identical in the rephotograph, we would

Notes for this essay will be found on page 27.

above
William Henry Jackson

White House Mountain, Elk Lake. 1873
United States Geological Survey, Denver

below
Mark Klett and JoAnn Verburg
for the Rephotographic Survey Project

Snow Mass Mountain, Geneva Lake, Colorado.
1977
Courtesy of the artists

expect to see some clear evidence of the passage of 100 years of time. But the visual evidence provided by the RSP pairs proved more problematic than expected.

An eccentric, but revealing, case in point is the pair consisting of Jackson's *White House Mountain, Elk Lake,* 1873, with the RSP's *Snow Mass Mountain, Geneva Lake,* 1977. In the intervening century, both the mountain and the lake have changed names, but the only dramatic visual difference between the two photographs is the disappearance of a rather large boulder. Not recorded by the camera in 1977, but noted by JoAnn Verburg of the RSP during shooting, was the fact that, "Ironically, as we set up our equipment for this comparison, which shows such minimal change, there were brightly-colored tents, fishermen, and back-packers playing radios and eating junk food behind us."[3] Although there are other pairs in the RSP work that show direct evidence of 20th century change within the photographic frame (a road for cars now parallel to older railroad tracks, a river valley now dammed into a lake), overall there is no single before / after analysis that emerges as we look at this particular stereographic *déjà vu;* neither consistent evidence of a march of progress nor pictures of Dorian Gray. The complication is clearly one of scale, partly spatial, but mostly temporal. Spatially, we are most often presented with vast natural environments. Whenever 19th century cultural baggage does invade the frame (a person, tent, etc.), it is most often consciously there for "scale," i.e., to be dwarfed by what surrounds it. Had the original Survey photographers taken only close-ups of single objects, the chances would be greater that the rephotograph would be unambiguous in its update: that is, whether the object is still there, shows specific signs of aging, or is gone. But the vastness of space described by the great majority of the RSP pairs makes for matching elements that are gargantuan in size as well as complex and subtle in their ecology: the outline of mountain ranges, high cliffs, deep valleys.

The temporal questions raised by these doubles are, however, far more elusive to deal with than the physical ones. This is due not so much to a limitation of photographic documentation as to our limited ability to quantify "raw" time. When asked to think of 100 years ago, we most often do so in the most unproblematic measurement terms: simply subtracting one from the 100s column on a mental calendar, and remembering who was President, or recalling some event or network of related events we know took place around that time. Likewise, if we are asked to describe the difference between now and 100 years ago, we most often isolate some unproblematic line of measurement: people live longer, bombs are bigger, communication is faster. But how can we characterize what happens to, and seize a mental image of, a vast remote space as it plods through a 100-year period? Our chronological clock reads "100 years" without ambiguity; but faced with these pairs, our internal time-piece spins erratically, unsure of its direction.

This unanticipated result of the RSP image pairs reflects the same set of complications contained in all time-machine stories from the sci-fi pulps to Mark Twain's *A Connecticut Yankee in King Arthur's Court.* In these stories, any location in time must also be a location in a physical and cultural space. They assume that the time-machine is also a "location-machine," since getting back there is only half the problem. For obvious narrative purposes, both the physical and cultural locations are generally unproblematic— these stories do not pose the dilemmas of (1) one goes back 100 years only to find that one's foot is "now" inside a large tree, or (2) one goes back 100 years but lands in rural, 19th-century Bolivia, spending the rest of one's life tolerated as an eccentric by friendly natives, babbling in an unknown tongue about automobiles and laser-beams. The first type of problem (left foot in tree), was occasionally encountered in the RSP travels. At one site, after a long and difficult journey, the rephotographic vantage point was found to be directly in front of a small bush, blocking the camera lens perfectly. After much philosophical discussion, a couple of years

were conveniently subtracted for the benefit of the rephotograph as the offending bush was pushed to the ground, out of the frame and out of history. The second problem (observing a past culture and time from a contemporary frame of reference) is a more general one. However, its manifestation in the RSP pairs is everpresent, as we are continually referencing the original to its update, and vice versa. The ways in which two photographs of identical vantage point inform each other across a chasm of 100 years time is at the crux of the RSP work. Jackson's photographs were made to describe natural wonders for an enthusiastic 19th-century audience; however, when the RSP pairs them off with a contemporary update, the resulting doubles tell us as much about how we measure time as how we measure mountains.

It would be instructive at this point to consider some photographic counter-examples to the temporal descriptions posited by the RSP. The doubles of Frank Gohlke and Bill Ganzel encompass time periods of one year and four decades respectively, but as we have seen with the RSP, absolute clock time is not necessarily of much help to us as we try to establish a clear relationship between the two photographs. Unlike the RSP, Gohlke's doubles encompass a discrete "event," the city of Wichita Falls' response to a natural disaster. Gohlke photographed the effects of a tornado on a suburban section of the city in 1979, and then returned to those same sites in 1980. The one-year time period between Gohlke's verifiably before/after photographs is arbitrary but relatively digestable as an experience. These doubles often lack the strict "transparent-overlay" appearance of the RSP pairs, but what is so frustratingly absent from the RSP, i.e., explicit visual evidence for determining the passage of cultural time, is the very subject of Gohlke's *Aftermath* series. We are often surprised at the result: these pairs are as much "after/before" as they are "before/after," as restoration takes the form of suburban replication. In some pairs, the repair is not complete, or has been redirected or

postponed; other images show such total change that even site recognition is difficult. The most revealing of these doubles, however, are ones in which some specific element either does recur or is replicated: the decorative windows of a tract house, the utilitarian structure of a liquor store sign, the relative proportions of home/yard/lot. This return to "normal" in the "after" image is in every case dramatized by its relation to the "before" photograph, an excruciatingly exact, even elegant rendition of every twisted tornado-wrought detail. Poignantly, we travel from images of massive destruction, of powerful, unleashed Nature, to ones showing the visual banality of normalcy, a dull rebirth in which it seems only the trees remember the world-changing force of the tornado. (These trees contrast with the streetlight and one-way sign of another pair, which have popped right back up one year later.) There is a sense of closure in all this, but one reminiscent of the realization often sparked by the staccato calendar of a family album: somehow we got from A to B, life went on and goes on despite our inability to fully acknowledge or track it. In Gohlke's pairs, as we move back and forth from disaster to recovery, we are made aware of the inadequacy of any before/after equation for describing all that we think and feel as we look from the first to the second. They make us feel a bit like Job, at the end of his trials and tribulations, searching the faces of his "restored" sons and daughters for some clues to the deeper nature of the changes between their past and present selves.

Bill Ganzel's point of departure is a man-made rather than natural disaster: the Great Depression of the 1930s. His raw material consists of photographs selected from the files of the Farm Security Administration, paired with a contemporary photograph of the same person or place. His doubles are the most immediately fascinating since they begin with source photographs that are both familiar and of consequence to a very large audience. Because of the status of his source material, and because of the nature of what they picture, the resulting pairs raise additional issues. The basis for the RSP

rephotography, the identity of vantage point, may be difficult to achieve, but is conceptually very clean. Ganzel's matching element is sometimes a location, but most often it is a person. In contrast to Gohlke's doubles, the series of events that spawned the original FSA photograph was infinitely more complex in its destruction than any tornado, and in contrast to the RSP's work, more explicitly cultural than any mountain range. Ganzel's pairs cannot impart a sense of closure as Gohlke's pairs do, since no single event is bracketed. Similarly, his rephotograph cannot meaningfully employ an RSP-style duplication of physical vantage point without generating a kind of bizarre parody. Instead, Ganzel follows Roy Stryker, the official head and guiding light of the FSA photographic project, in emphasizing the totality of the FSA work as its measure of meaning. Presenting his work, Ganzel quotes Stryker: "I wanted to do a pictorial encyclopedia of American agriculture... In truth, I think the work we did can be appreciated only when the collection is considered as a whole."[4] Ganzel, in his rephotography, is not simply collecting more specimens to add to that whole, but is instead attempting to give it an additional dimension, to add the perspective of a different point in time to parts of the collection's whole. The update is sometimes discouraging: although some have recovered into a middle or lower middle class status, a substantial number of the nation's most economically disadvantaged citizens of the 1930s have remained so into the late seventies. And they are older.

'While only a select few can understand the discoveries of the physicists, or the exact measurements of the engineers, everyone can understand a clock.'

'Bring me men to match my measurements...'

We periodically hear impassioned calls for a "new" FSA project; the reasons no new one has formed are obviously complex. Certainly one reason is that our primary source of photographic reporting has long since shifted from the photo-journalist's still camera to the ENG video camera of broadcast television. However, any thoughts about "doing it again" with still photography most often start with the assumption that certain structures of the original FSA project must be replicated that in fact needn't be. By starting off with the duplication of the subject matter of individual photographs of the FSA rather than trying to duplicate its procedural style, Ganzel implicitly challenges the notion that the furtherance of the FSA's work must necessarily consist of a modern version of FSA structure: bodies of work created by individual artist-photographers who cover the country and divide it into territories, locating their particular aesthetic conceits somewhere in contemporary society. Instead, and in the same spirit as the RSP, Ganzel attempts to further understand an existing body of work by experimenting with a rephotographic methodology. He doesn't try to match the individual power and iconographic status of the FSA image he has chosen to rephotograph, and in any case, his interests do not lie in that kind of aesthetic task. Instead, his work asks at least two questions: (1) how can we measure cultural change from the point of view of an individual human lifetime—a question he enhances by using captions taken from interviews with persons in or involved with the original photograph—and, more generally, (2) how can we presently understand ("re-cognize") a famous image from the past when the complex cultural context in which it was born and to which it refers has itself been inevitably transformed?

The photographic doubles of Eve Sonneman, although not "rephotographic" in the strict RSP sense, are important counterpoints to the work previously discussed. Her work is also in the form of two prints displayed together, and the resulting pairs have the look of consecutive frames from a 35mm contact sheet. In contrast to the RSP, Ganzel, and Gohlke, Sonneman's doubles measure time with a rubber ruler, existing in the free floating time zone of short-term memory. The "event" they encompass, and the time in which they take place are unquantifiable, but there are always enough clues to let us know that the location of both photographs is in the same general place. The time period of the RSP pairs is exactly fixed in calendar years, as is the vantage point, but the time portrayed is ponderous, grand, and ultimately incomprehensible. Sonneman's pairs, by contrast, present subjective time/place relationships, but as a consequence, allow a rich and free arena within which we can move between the two photographs in our effort to connect them. This travel is subjective, but not arbitrary or surreal. Rather, there is the feeling of the common human experience of suddenly "waking up" after having found oneself staring off into space: two points of conscious notation that bracket an unquantifiable experience. The pairs are not dreamlike, but they recall the delusive memory of our dreams—the mad scramble in the split second in which we regain consciousness when we arrange and rearrange fragmentary images into the best possible narrative of what we have seen while asleep. This fluid and subjective sense of narrative connection in Sonneman's pairs posits a complex, but intimately human, time frame.

Since all photographs occur at a specific time, correlating them on the basis of some time sequence is quite natural—a family snapshot album may be an irregular calendar, but it can still comprise a "complete" and evocative image. However, structuring a more rigid correlation between photographs and the times at which they occur has been an intriguing possibility from the birth of photography onward. The most literal correlation occurs, of course, when the camera is linked to the most literal time-marker, the clock. Eadweard Muybridge, the pioneering sequence photographer of the 1870s and 80s, began his famous horse-in-motion experiments in 1872 with only one camera. He attempted to catch a discrete point in the horse's running cycle by relying on his considerable, but all-too-human ability to catch the right moment for exposure. By 1878, he was not only using a bank of twelve cameras to photograph the entire running cycle, but had necessarily changed to a physical, contingent shutter trigger—a series of twelve wires stretched perpendicular to the path of motion at equal intervals, each one connected to the shutter mechanism of a different camera. But this triggering system, although mechanical, was still potentially irregular since it was totally dependent on the movement of the horse. Muybridge's next step was crucial: he changed from a contingent trigger to a predetermined, mechanical one when he began using a clockwork mechanism to fire the shutters in a programmable sequence, a sequence totally independent of both subjective human judgement and the phenomenon being recorded. Once he replaced wire-tripping with the obliviously regular sweep of a rotating electrical wipe contact, lens and clock were merged into one dispassionate scan. This made his studies both "scientific" and visually self-contained. Significantly, Muybridge's clock/lens "machine" was perfected concurrently with a host of other electromagnetically-based analog devices: the telephone in 1876; the phonograph in 1877; the microphone in 1878.

The life span of the "events" that Muybridge photographed in subsequent animal and human locomotion studies was most often the multi-second repeatable cycle variety: man/woman jumps, runs, tumbles; horse/dog/bird gallops, sprints, flaps. The exceptions to this general pattern in his work are the images contemporary photographers most often gravitate towards, images in which something strange or unlikely is happening: woman pretends to spank child; figure receives shocks while sitting. But these examples, as enigmatic as they are, are of interest precisely because they brown-out the voltage to Muybridge's clock; they refuse to be encapsulated within, or explicated by, a rigid time frame. His typical locomotion study, however, encompasses a cadence cycle, a unit of continuous activity that provides glimpses into a familiar, repeatable, and nameable time scale (one big zoetrope: Abe Edgington trots and trots; Daisy jumps and jumps; active verbs are easier to both say and see). Yet even this continuous-cycle type is not free of complication, as demonstrated by *Indian Elephant Ambling,* which is difficult to see as one cycle, or feel as a cadence; it's easier to see it as a static, repetitious block of postage stamps. Muybridge's locomotion studies are revealing for a certain range of action, but it is obvious what he would *not* train his multiple timed cameras on: a dead horse decomposing, some children at unspecified play; a monk achieving Nirvana. Muybridge's studies gain their power by limiting themselves to a quantifiable cadence of activity, and of necessity, a relatively short and conceptually digestible time period. This is a powerful, but rigidly defined methodology. Muybridge, unlike the legions compiling family snapshot albums, was not interested in understanding time as a function of activity, but rather in measuring activity against an absolute time standard.

Bill Ganzel

Florence Thompson and her daughters Norma Rydlewski (in front), Katherine McIntosh and Ruby Sprague, at Norma's house.
Modesto, California
June 1979
Courtesy of the artist

Dorothea Lange

Migrant Mother [Florence Thompson with her daughters: Norma, in her arms; Katherine, left; and Ruby].
Nipomo, California
March 1936
Library of Congress, Washington, D.C.

"She worked hard, brought us up and kept us together. We all have good jobs and we all own our own homes. And none of us have ever been in trouble."

Katherine McIntosh (daughter of Florence Thompson)

"Women, especially, would give to their children and they would do without. When we were growing up, if mother weighed 100 pounds, she was fat."

Ruby Sprague (daughter of Florence Thompson)

"I left Oklahoma in 1925 and went to California. The Depression hit about 1931, just about the time them girls' [her daughters'] dad died. I was 28 years old, and I had five kids and one on the way. You couldn't get no work and what you could, it was very hard and cheap. I'd leave home before daylight and come home after dark. Grapes, 'taters, peas, whatever I was doing. Barely made enough each day to buy groceries that night. I'd pick four or five hundred pounds of cotton every day. I didn't even weigh 100 pounds. We just existed; we survived, let's put it that way.

"When Steinbeck wrote *Grapes of Wrath* about those people living under the bridge at Bakersfield —At one time we lived under that bridge. It was the same story. Didn't even have a tent then, just a ratty old quilt. I walked from what they'd call the Hoover camp at the bridge to 'way down on First Street to work in a restaurant for 50 cents a day and left-overs. They'd give me what was left over to take home, sometimes two water buckets full. I had six children to feed at that time."

Florence Thompson

Although Muybridge's studies were used primarily as a way to observe and quantify animal and human locomotion, the technique itself suggests using the information derived to modify the nature of what was originally measured—a tool for change as well as observation. Such was the purpose of Frank and Lillian Gilbreth's time/motion studies conducted during the 1910s and 20s in this country.[5] In these studies, workers of various callings were placed against background grids à la Muybridge and their tasks tracked by still and motion picture cameras in order to discover the most "efficient," i.e., verifiably profitable, work motions. Like Muybridge's work, these time/motion studies merged the camera's rationalization of space with the clock's rationalization of time, but did so with an even more literal time/image mechanism —the motion picture camera. Cinema was now being deployed not merely to provide diversion on weekends but to scrutinize and quantify work habits during the week. This dehumanizing potential of the clock/lens, when applied wholesale and single-mindedly to human activity, was a disturbing possibility from Muybridge and Marey onward. Ironically, perhaps the most memorable call to arms against the "real time" of synchronized clock/lens was made from an aesthetic, not humanist, basis. Anton Bragaglia, a member of the Futurist movement, commented in 1913 on Marey's chronophotography of some thirty years earlier: "To put it crudely, chronophotography could be compared to a clock on the face of which only the half-hours are marked, cinematography to one on which the minutes too are indicated, and Photodynamism [Bragaglia's own "expressively" stepped multiple exposures] to a third on which are marked not only the seconds, but also the intermomental fractions existing in the passages between seconds."[6]

While Bragaglia was reacting most immediately to Marey and the cinematic camera, his suspicion that the clock—and the way we measure generally—withholds as much as it reveals goes back at least as far as the 5th century B.C. with Zeno of Elea and his famous paradoxes of time and motion, the best-known of which is the race of Achilles and the Tortoise. For this seemingly uneven race, the Tortoise gets a head-start. The Tortoise moves very slowly, but before Achilles can catch up and pass him, he must first cover half the distance to the Tortoise. After that, he must then cover half of the remaining distance, then half of that, and so on, in an infinitely regressing unbreakable cycle. We know, of course, that Achilles is capable of winning easily, and that the race cannot go on forever. This leaves us with the disturbing possibility that something is wrong or incomplete about the way we "objectively" measure time and motion. The root complication is with the concept of the infinitesimal, and although the calculus of Newton and Leibnitz in the 17th century sounded the beginning of the end for the race and its paradox, it wasn't until the 19th century that key concepts in modern calculus (functions, limits, the derivative, the integral, convergence of sequence and series) allowed Achilles to finally win conceptually.[7] However, the resolution of the paradox by 19th-century mathematicians was quite humble when translated into a racing score-sheet: object A is at point B at time T; the why and what it means was left to others. The mathematicians were not trying to define reality, they were simply trying to make an abstract way of thinking internally consistent.

The Gilbreth's "one best way," the goal of their time/motion studies, reflected the values of their industrial backers rather than the dictates of modern mathematics, just as Bragaglia's Photodynamism reflected a Futurist aesthetic in its attempt to recalibrate the face of the clock. The doubles of the RSP, Gohlke, Ganzel and Sonneman place their emphasis less on the sufficiency or insufficiency of the clock mechanism than on exploring the process of correlating photographs in reference to the human sense of time—all kinds of time. The four bodies of work in question do not simply show four different speeds of the same time-lapse camera; rather, they demonstrate that there are distinct time-spaces we can point to and contemplate through the photographic process, as we blend short-term memory, long-term memory, and history in an attempt to bridge the two photographs. These photographic doubles start with one of the more fundamental human perceptual tasks: how do we distinguish between similars? Beginning there, we base our distinction in reference to time but in terms of memory, and neither mathematicians nor mechanical engineers have yet arrived at a meaningful calculus of human memory.

In this context, the RSP doubles are intimately related to the other pairs in the presentation of similars between which the viewer must distinguish in reference to time and memory, but in doing so, also take the most extreme position. The reason the RSP pairs encompass such a problematic time-space has to do, of course, with what is being "matched." Since the pairs are not just "impressions" of the 19th and 20th centuries at a common site, and since looking at the two together is not like examining two comparable cultural artifacts from 1873 and 1977—such as two newspapers, two paintings, or even two maps—we have pairs of similars that provide us with truly unique juxtapositions. The way the pairs coincide is as relentless and literal as an astronomer's sextant, but the cadence, the cycle, the "gesture" of the time between the two photographs is unmatchable to any human-scale memory or experience, as well as ambiguous in its relation to history.

But the RSP's replication of vantage point also demonstrates something else, something that harks back to Brassai's observation on the dual function of all photographs. Jackson's photographs, as "art," have been described as having "honest clarity of vision...a tribute to the subject itself, and to the sensitivity of the photographer and his ability to capture natural beauty in a straightforward photograph, with clear vision and direct technique...[Jackson] *lets the subject say what it has to say,* rather than what the photographer has to say about it."[8] [Italics mine.] These comments typify Brassai's duality of the living second and the daughter of the beaux arts, i.e., a simultaneous claim on the part of the photographer for both "true expression" and "objective description." But what is the source of these two qualities in Jackson's photographs? Whereas objective (at least optical) description is certainly in the eye of Jackson's camera, the truth of his expression might best be assigned to the eye of the dominant cultural sense of what constitutes a well-composed landscape image specifically, and to a Manifest Destiny sense of grandeur generally. (It's beautiful— and it's ours.) Jackson's specific framing of his subject matter was necessarily informed by his 19th-century compositional sensibilities; because the RSP found the exact point in space from which Jackson made his photograph, but by design was not subject to the same conventions as he was, what we get from these doubles is a look at Jackson's "subject matter" without simultaneously replicating his "composition." The RSP has distinguished the rephoto-graph from Jackson's original by implicitly photographing the time between them. Put another way, the "compositional" purity of the original Jackson photograph is jarred loose from its "subject matter" by the effects of time, as evidenced by the rephotograph. The rephotograph, by itself, would tell us very little. It's the two taken together, and the triangulation we make between them, that both constitute the measure of its photographic meaning and inform its 20th century aesthetic.

This triangulation is a demonstration of something that is fundamental to all photographs, but difficult to ever show explicitly: that the meaning of the photograph does not reside in its physical structure, but rather in the dynamic and negotiating interaction between ourselves, our culture, and the image in question. This demonstration is most vivid in the work of the RSP because the time-space context it describes is the most exaggerated. As a strategy, however, the triangulation of doubles to describe a time-space context is equally at work in the Gohlke, Ganzel and Sonneman doubles. They are all efforts to heighten our awareness of the fundamental duality of photographic function described by Brassai at the opening of this essay. Further, the general principle of distinction between similars—the fundamental basis of these doubles—is expanded and redirected by the other photographers in this exhibition. They employ such diverse strategies as the use of linear sequence, composite multiple, and grid-array, and take as subject matter such diverse areas as a personal time-space (Parada), a class of objects/functions (Bechers), or a spatial description (Flick). Underlying all these strategies and different subjects, however, is the basic notion that while we as viewers most often focus on a single photograph at a time, photographs are themselves seldom solitary or reclusive. Photographs tend to gather in groups, whether by design or chance, and any understanding of photography must include an understanding of photographic discourse, i.e., the way photographs are put together to convince, convey, document, or persuade. A more complex awareness of photographs as a means for making and manipulating meaning in various contexts has emerged since the beginning of photography. If for no other reason than their mere plenitude, we can scarcely think of photographs as separate from the picture environments they have created—and inhabit. Photographs are particularly rich in resonances, just as they are provocative of associations: one image may "quote" or reinforce another in a developing network of connections by which the ecology of a picture environment is defined. This contextual reality of photographic history is a continuous interaction between one photograph and others, between the bondage and liberation of conventions, and between the changing circumstances of a particular culture and time.

One final note on the RSP in this regard: the RSP, like Jackson himself, kept diaristic notations on events surrounding and including their picture-making. One is particularly revealing. When the RSP first relocated the site of Jackson's famous *Mountain of the Holy Cross* they found the snowfall to be substantially less than on the comparable date the year Jackson had photographed it. When Jackson was there, the snow-packed cracks in the mountain formed the awe inspiring crucifix shape that is now so familiar to us; but by the seventh decade of the 20th century, the mountain's majesty could only manage a hesitant apostrophe mark. The *"Mountain of the Holy Apostrophe"* they jokingly called it, as they hiked back down the rugged terrain. Who knows, perhaps the mountain was 'saying what it had to say' as articulately on that day in the late 20th century as it had been for Jackson more than 100 years before.

P.B.

1. Sam Walter Foss, *Whiffs from Wild Meadows* (Boston: Lothrop, Lee and Shepard Co., n.d. [c 1895]), p. 444.

2. *Brassai* (New York: Museum of Modern Art, 1968), p. 13.

3. JoAnn Verburg, "Rephotographing Jackson," *Afterimage* 6, nos. 1 & 2 (Summer 1978), p. 6.

4. Quoted in Bill Ganzel, "Familiar Faces, Familiar Places," *Exposure* 16, no. 3 (Fall 1978), p. 50.

5. Bruce Kaiper, "The Cyclograph and the Work Motion Model," in *Still Photography, the Problematic Model*, eds. Lew Thomas and Peter D'Agostino (San Francisco: NSF Press, 1981), pp. 56-63.

6. Quoted in Caroline Tisdall and Angelo Bozzolla, *Futurism*, (London: Thames and Hudson, 1977), p. 138.

7. Wesley C. Salmon, *Space, Time and Motion: A Philosophical Introduction*, (Encino: Dickenson, 1975), p. 35. The entire 2nd chapter, "A Contemporary Look at Zeno's Paradoxes," is of interest in this regard.

8. William L. Brocker, "The Photographs of William H. Jackson," in Beaumont Newhall & Diana E. Edkins, *William H. Jackson* (New York/Fort Worth: Morgan & Morgan/Amon Carter Museum, 1974), pp. 19-20.

above
Timothy H. O'Sullivan

Quartz Mill near Virginia City. 1868
United States Geological Survey, Denver

below
Timothy H. O'Sullivan

Green River Buttes, Green River, Wyoming. 1872
United States Geological Survey, Denver

The RSP photographs deal as much with some-times erroneous expectations of before and after as they do with the traditions of landscape and documentation. In this particular array of four, the viewer is invited to cross-compare the photographs.

Timothy H. O'Sullivan   **Timothy H. O'Sullivan**

above
Mark Klett
for the Rephotographic Survey Project

Site of the Gould and Curry Mine, Virginia City,
Nevada. 1979
Courtesy of the artist

below
Mark Klett and Gordon Bushaw
for the Rephotographic Survey Project

Castle Rock, Green River, Wyoming. 1979
Courtesy of the artist

above
Frank Gohlke

4673 Woodlawn, looking west, June 1980, from
Aftermath: The Wichita Falls Tornado, 1982
Courtesy of the artist

below
Frank Gohlke

4673 Woodlawn, looking west, April 15, 1979,
from *Aftermath: The Wichita Falls Tornado,* 1982
Courtesy of the artist

Aftermath: The Wichita Falls Tornado *is a series
of photographs dealing with the destruction and
rebuilding of Wichita Falls, Texas. The issue,
however, is not history but rather our inability to
distinguish clearly which is before and what is
after. This page intentionally inverts the actual time
sequence and creates a reading more closely
resembling one's expectations of before and after.*

Frank Gohlke

Frank Gohlke

1600 Block, Aldrich Avenue, looking east,
April 14, 1979, from *Aftermath: The Wichita Falls*
Tornado, 1982
Courtesy of the artist

Frank Gohlke

1600 Block, Aldrich Avenue, looking east,
June 1980, from *Aftermath: The Wichita Falls*
Tornado, 1982
Courtesy of the artist

Arthur Rothstein

Vernon Evans [and] *his family of Lemmon, South Dakota, on Highway #10, left the grasshopper-ridden and drought stricken area for a new start in Oregon or Washington. They expect to arrive at Yakima, Washington in time for hop-picking. They live in a tent and make about 200 miles a day in a Model-T Ford.*

Missoula (vicinity), Montana
July [18,] 1936
Library of Congress, Washington, D.C.

Vernon Evans on the farm his father home-
steaded and to which Vernon returned after
nine years in Oregon.
Lemmon, South Dakota
July 18, 1977
Courtesy of the artist

"Well, we was all without jobs here at the time. The jobs was so few and far between that you couldn't buy a job. We had friends that we knew out in Oregon, and we decided we was going to go out there and see if we could find work. We had $54 between the five of us when we started out, and when we got to Oregon, I think we had about $16 left. We had absolutely no idea what we was going to do.

"We got out around Missoula, and we was having a good time. There was this car sitting along 'side the road and a guy sleeping in it, so we honked and hollered at him, having a big time. Pretty soon this car was after us. Well, we seen he had an emblem on the side of the car, and we'd heard they was sending 'em (the migrants) back, wasn't letting 'em go through. So, we thought, 'here's where we go back home.' He motioned for us to pull over. Anyhow, he come over and introduced himself— Arthur Rothstein was his name—and he said he was with the Resettlement Administration. This 'Oregon or Bust' on the back end was what took his eye. He asked us if we cared if he took some pictures of us. That fall or winter, why, these pictures started showing up in the different magazines and papers.

"In the winter of '45, my father passed away. I come back and kind of took over the farm and helped out here. I've been here ever since. We've had our ups and downs, I guess. I've been hailed out probably five, six times, and dried out three, four years, and one year we rusted out."

Vernon Evans

Frank Gohlke

***Maplewood Avenue, near Sikes Senter Mall,
looking northeast, April 14, 1979,*** from *Aftermath:
The Wichita Falls Tornado,* 1982
Courtesy of the artist

Frank Gohlke

Maplewood Avenue, near Sikes Senter Mall,
looking northeast, June 1980, from *Aftermath:*
The Wichita Falls Tornado, 1982
Courtesy of the artist

above
Frank Gohlke

View of Faith Village from Kiwanis Park, looking east, April 15, 1979, from *Aftermath: The Wichita Falls Tornado,* 1982
Courtesy of the artist

below
Arthur Rothstein

Wife of a Farmsteader [*Mrs. Harvey Taft*].
Falls City Farmstead, Nebraska
May 1936
Library of Congress, Washington, D.C.

"I've enjoyed it all. I wouldn't have missed it for anything, and I wouldn't want to go through it again. It got to where you couldn't buy a job in the thirties when the Depression hit—got rough. It got to where I was working for a fellow for a dollar a day putting in about 14 hours a day. He comes to me and wanted to hire me for the season. He said he'd give me $17 a month. He says he could hire a man for that.

"I says, 'Well, you'd better go hire him because,' I says, 'I can't. Less than a dollar a day, my family can't live. I know, I tried it too long.'

"So he says, 'What will you do?'

"I says, 'I can sign on the relief.' So I did. I got $2.44 a day on relief and a grocery order. Then they built this project here and I was selected for one of the families to move on this farmstead. Ten families moved on this 80 acres and had about seven acres apiece, vegetable farming. We built the caves after we moved here.

"After four years we quit vegetable farming and they organized us into a nonstock co-op. But the other men didn't co-op with me. They wouldn't help me when the hay needed put up, they didn't help

above
Frank Gohlke

View of Faith Village from Kiwanis Park, Looking east, June 1980, from *Aftermath: The Wichita Falls Tornado,* 1982
Courtesy of the artist

below
Bill Ganzel

Arthur Rothstein in the "cave" on Harvey Taft's farm. Harvey was one of the original members of the FSA-sponsored cooperative farmstead and bought most of the land and buildings when the program ended in the early forties. North of Falls City, Nebraska
September 1979
Courtesy of the artist

shock the grain. I blew up. I says, 'I'm done with this co-op.' But some big shots came here and they wanted to sell me a farm out of this. So, I told my wife, I says, 'We'd better just stay right here.' And we stayed.

"I sold out when I was 65, 14 years ago. I sold out to my son Cleo here and just reserved my home. I don't own a thing but my household goods and my automobile. I got everything the way I wanted it when I got old, only that I'm left alone.

Harvey Taft

Frank Gohlke

View of Faith Village from Kiwanis Park, Looking east, June 1980, from *Aftermath: The Wichita Falls Tornado,* 1982
Courtesy of the artist

Bill Ganzel

Arthur Rothstein in the "cave" on Harvey Taft's farm. Harvey was one of the original members of the FSA-sponsored cooperative farmstead and bought most of the land and buildings when the program ended in the early forties. North of Falls City, Nebraska
September 1979
Courtesy of the artist

Eve Sonneman

Memory, New York. 1979
2 color prints mounted side-by-side
Courtesy of the artist and Castelli Graphics,
New York

Memory Warp II. 1980
25 prints mounted contiguously in five rows of five
Courtesy of the artist

In Esther Parada's Memory Warp series, the
persistence and fragility of human time appears in
a palimpsest, with personal articles layered over
a death mask photograph of the artist's father.
Superimposed images display both the passage
of time and our intimate involvement with it.

Esther Parada

Memory Warp III. 1980
25 prints mounted contiguously in five rows of five
Courtesy of the artist

Eve Sonneman

Newspaper, New York. 1980
2 color prints mounted side-by-side
Courtesy of the artist and Castelli Graphics,
New York

Eadweard Muybridge

Detail of ***Abe Edgington Trotting,*** from *The Horse in Motion,* 1879
Collection of R. Joseph and Elaine R. Monsen

Photographic "pages," whatever their scale, make us directly aware of the density of information that can be conveyed by visual means. Not only do we see, in a single scan, each component image, we apprehend, as a whole or gestalt, the pattern made by the photographic array as one composite picture.

Homologues appear, however, once any format or procedure is invoked, since what one actually sees in a full display discloses subtle similarities, not only from one image to another, but from aspects of images to other aspects, even in the same image. Thus, as a bat's wing is homologous to a mouse's foot, we may see more subtle resemblances between patterns of light, figures and grounds, or tonal variations, from one image to another or one array to another.

Order, as we apprehend it, therefore always involves us: what we see on the page, like what we see in the world, is subject to analysis, re-configuration, or re-cognition. It is never static. But when a photographer employs a definite procedure or follows a distinctive strategy as a means to investigate some part of visible reality, we are taken into the investigation as an implicit collaborator, since we will supply the coordinates in psychological reality.

Time, in this context, is bracketed out as an arbitrary variable: it is only the interval between images, between determinations of picture space. The Muybridge grid, now familiar as a graphic convention, but not a necessary point of reference for a pre-determined temporal interval, begins to function with the paradoxical liberation of a rule: one's freedom has value only within the confines of some set of conventions.

Operations of this kind are obviously complex, since they are implicit or actual transactions—first, between the photographer and some potential image source, and second, between the photographs and the viewer. As we have noted, the constant complication in transactions of both kinds is the variegated determination of a space/time manifold.

Graphic components, that is, are vehicles of significance, that we, as viewers, must first notice and fit into a pattern, in order to understand the picture. Sometimes, it is with an eerie sense of surprise that details in a display will activate our visual memories, and we will be reminded of images far removed, but clearly associated.

Repeat encounters with a photographic procedure or strategy, in turn, expand the space in which one can make coherent associations, and supply the basis for a visually intelligible map of one's own time and place, within a fuller macro-matrix of organic and cultural history.

Analysis comes into its own once the rule of time is relaxed, for the multiple relations that can appear within pictorial space, expanded to the area of a grid, or displaced into a sustained linear sequence, permit a dramatic increase in intensity, and a corresponding increase in coherence.

Perspective is established, for both the photographer and the viewer, by anticipations —"How will this look, as a photograph?"—or expectations—"Does this look like anything else?" For the photographer, expectation is more directly open, since it is the imaginative operation of projectively filling a blank space, either of a single frame or of a generalized format, according to some flexible plan.

Holographic images produce a similar psychological effect, by constructing associative networks in three dimensions; but photographic arrays presuppose our imaginative participation. The effect, while strange, is not mysterious: it only shows that "seeing" is an active process.

Initiates into any "order" find their way around by precedent and example. Since the example of Muybridge, the use of grids and extended sequences has become at once a principle of inquiry and a principle of order. In our time, it appears that the picture space has become again the radical ground of imagination.

Comprehension of a set of picture possibilities appears to be the main motive in this work; and as it unfolds, it carries us along in a remarkable intellectual voyage. In the remainder of this book, we will examine this pursuit of comprehension from several perspectives, by repeating the theme (and variations), of this collaborative survey.

Marion Faller and Hollis Frampton

Apple Advancing (var. "Northern Spy"), Number 782, "Sixteen Studies from *Vegetable Locomotion,"* 1975
Print from 12 negatives
Courtesy of the artists and Visual Studies
Workshop Gallery, Rochester

Eadweard Muybridge

Indian Elephant Ambling, Plate 733,
Animal Locomotion, 1887
Print from 24 negatives in three rows of eight
Sanford Family Collection,
Stanford University Museum of Art

In Plato's *Republic,* Socrates defines as "provocatives" those subjects where "perception no more manifests one thing than its contrary" (*Republic,* 523c). And while Plato had no patience for the makers of images as makers of illusion (as is evident, for example, in the *Phaedo, Republic* book X, and the *Sophist*), he surely would have found Marion Faller and Hollis Frampton provocative.

In *Apple Advancing,* the joke is obvious enough, as we appear to have motion in a subject that has no power for it, just as we find the motion proceeding not across the reference grid in the background, but away from it, toward us. Whether we might be about to eat the apple or vice versa is not certain; but once we come to the end of amusement, these questions become analytically interesting.

Rotating the expected pictorial axis of motion, for example, exploits the simple fact that relative size and distance are correlative perceptual clues, without which we would have difficulty in perceiving either depth or motion. Simple as this is, however, it immediately alters an apparently extraneous condition—which is our own affective, psychological response. When objects pass serenely before us, left to right, we appear to occupy a privileged position, at a safe, spectatorly distance. It flatters our sense of being "objective" observers of a scene. But when the object appears to be coming directly toward us, even if that object is only an apple, we are put on alert. Perhaps in this case, we might look around this vegetable garden for a suspicious looking serpent.

Yet for present purposes, the more interesting fact is more abstract. In this, as in other cases, irony results when our expectations are thwarted or reversed; and parody in these terms is just irony made mildly aggressive. But in the reversal of expectations, fundamental operations appear all the more clearly. Thus, if a photographer maintains a constant camera position, against a constant background, apparent motion is comprehensible as an object following a vector. Motion is the trace of the vector, while sequential images provide

the sample of states which describe it. The abstract vector is then interpretable as a trajectory, and the space/time manifold is neatly packaged and delivered as a record of an "event."

Less technically, we do a kind of informal trigonometry in reading photographic arrays: we triangulate, in the expectation that our attention will be foregrounded upon the object which changes. By simple changes of orientation, or by inversions of expectations about objects undergoing some change of state, such operations and conventions (which are ordinarily automatic and unremarked) are themselves foregrounded, and objects appear to remain constant.

In Muybridge's *Indian Elephant Ambling,* for example, we can tell that this noble pachyderm changes state, but he is so huge and ponderous that the "event" is oddly suspended. In this case, it is as if Muybridge, obsessionally following his own program, verged on a parody of himself—or nature determined to parody him by offering a subject that acts on a much more leisurely scale of time, just as he dwarfs the measuring grid.

Be that as it may, whenever our "normal" sense of time or space is attenuated or disrupted, we become, as it were, formalists in spite of ourselves. Attention shifts to image aspects, patterns of "composition," detailed interplays of light and figure. But when such control is exercised by a photographer, picture space does become radical, as it opens a space for contemplation.

In these triangulating operations, of camera position, background, and figure, artistic control is the precise control of context. "Context" is, etymologically, a "weaving together"; by determining precisely what will be woven together in an integrated display, the photographer also sets conditions for viewer response.

Marion Faller and Hollis Frampton

Gourds vanishing (var. "Mixed Ornamental"),
Number 14, "Sixteen Studies from *Vegetable Locomotion*," 1975
Print from 12 negatives
Courtesy of the artists and Visual Studies
Workshop Gallery, Rochester

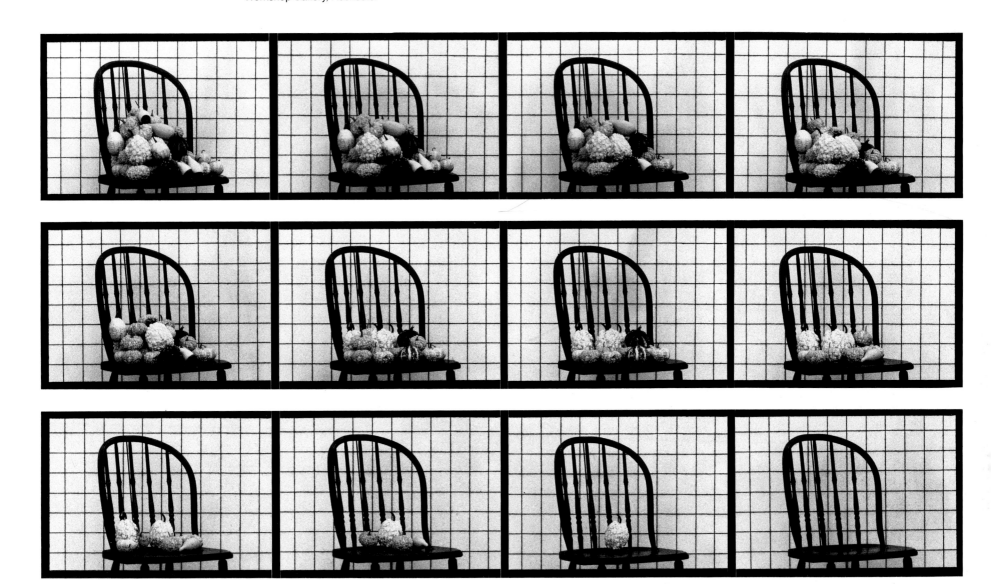

Bernd and Hilla Becher

Detail of *Cooling Towers.* 1978
16 prints mounted separately and displayed in two rows of eight
Collection of Bing Wright

Grids provide a framework for the presentation of ideas, but individual elements may not represent the intention of the whole. In the detail of Bernd and Hilla Becher's Cooling Towers reproduced below, the "element," once isolated, becomes an independent photograph, and it is no longer obvious that it is a fragment of a larger whole.

In the work of Bernd and Hilla Becher, for example, certain factors, especially camera position and the tone (or absence) of the horizon or background, are rigorously controlled to add to the monumentality of the objects foregrounded in each print in the array. Doing so, they achieve not just the austere look of a neutral "document," but an immensely powerful confrontation with the objects photographed—artifacts of industry, rapidly being supplanted, but all the more interesting on that account. For these are not, by and large, machines or pieces of apparatus that enter our daily lives—and if they do, they are there on a scale that precludes more than one being in your neighborhood.

Thus, these "documents" become resolutely abstract studies of "objecthood." That is, the change foregrounded by triangulation is a change in the particular identity of the thing photographed. We have no trouble forming the general concept of a "cooling tower"; but when we see four or sixteen of them side by side, each clearly a "cooling tower," and each clearly different from the others, we enter, by a visual door, the arena of philosophical disquisition. Sameness and difference are here woven together with consummate skill; and both modern nominalists, arguing that "universals" or "generals" are only artifacts of names, and modern realists, arguing for their meta-physical existence, might well be confounded by this visual presentation of the issue.

By means of the camera, it becomes clear that even such venerable philosophical debates, presuming to address issues of ultimate reality, are themselves the artifact of wholly verbal triangulation. In a photographic matrix, metaphysics vanishes, while the provocation of co-resident sameness and difference persists, not as the invitation to a debate about "reality" vs. "appearance," but a declaration of the reality OF appearance. What remains problematic is the set of conventions we employ to mediate our claims to knowledge.

With objects, we may take images as the signature of their identity, and their identity, in turn, as pure idea. This returns us to the etymological sense of "idea," from the Greek, *eidos,* the look or appearance of a thing; but it radically complicates our sense of the relation between an "image" and an "idea," when the two appear to coincide.

Again, irony comes to the rescue whenever we are tempted to think that we can abstract ourselves as participants in what we see and know. We are always there, even when we forget it; and one salutary function of photographic arrays is to remind us of that fact.

Thus, in Gary Metz' series of photographs of the backs of people's heads, the austere objecthood we noted in the Bechers appears in a most unexpected context. We expect the identity of persons to be acknowledged first in their faces. (Parenthetically, the Greek word *eidos* was most commonly applied to the "look" in someone's countenance.) This is not necessary, as Metz shows; but the irony in this case is that the control of camera position and format, with a literal reversal of expectations by turning the subjects around, reminds us of both the conventionality of our 'eideas' and the psychological force of such conventions.

While many of us may be uncomfortable being photographed face front, in part because it is so difficult to maintain a reciprocal relation with the resulting fixed image, we may be more uncomfortable as viewers looking at the backs of people's heads, since these photographic subjects have become non-reciprocating objects. It is as if by reversing this pictorial convention, Metz puts the burden of transaction on the viewer, literally facing the same way as the subject. Who then is watching whom—or what?

Cooling Towers. 1978
16 prints mounted separately and displayed in two
rows of eight
Collection of Bing Wright

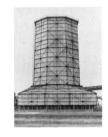

Bernd and Hilla Becher

Blast Furnace Heads. 1982
15 prints mounted separately and displayed in
three rows of five
Courtesy of the artists and Sonnabend Galley,
New York

Here, an area is isolated from Robbert Flick's Ocean 2 (see page 60). Unlike the Bechers', where the "detail" is itself another whole, the "detail" in Flick remains a part since the whole is an irreducible composite.

Robbert Flick,

Detail of ***Ocean 2.*** 1981
Print made from 81 negatives in nine rows of nine
Courtesy of the artist and Tortue Gallery, Santa
Monica

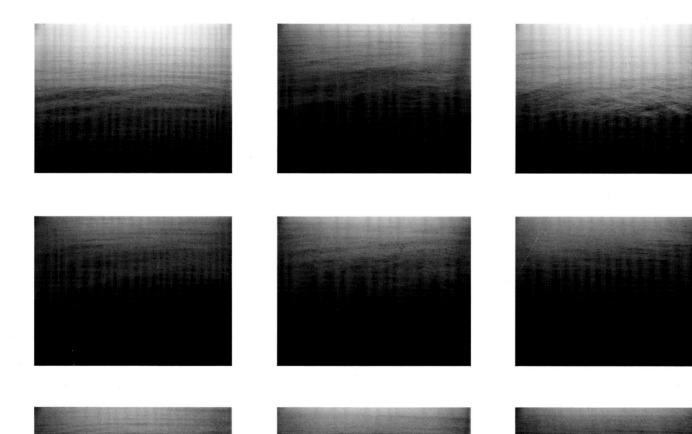

Gary Metz
4 prints from the series *Hair Piece ("Every Force Has Its Form"–Shaker Saying).* 1977-79
Courtesy of the artist

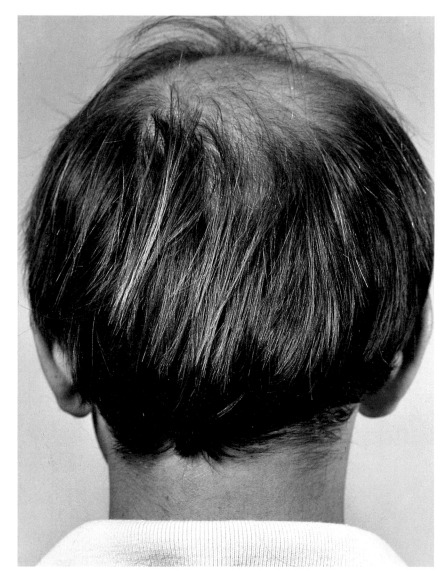 

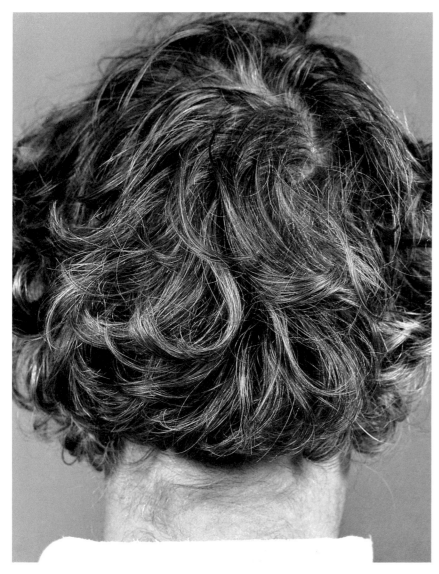

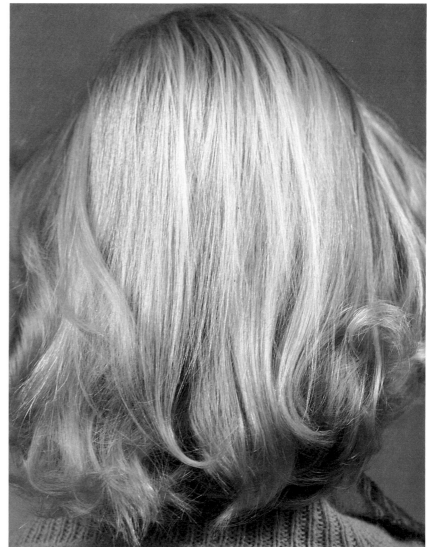

William S. Paris

Print "A-1" from *Observing Modifies the Observed.* 1981
Six rows of five prints
Courtesy of the artist

These five photographs are normally seen as a row (see pages 54-55). They have been rearranged to show how they function as independent photographs and as details taken out of context.

William S. Paris' *Observing Modifies the Observed* may be the most difficult work represented here to treat adequately in a book. It is uncommonly abstract, just as it is uncommonly powerful. Here, the principle of the array is implied by the title: it is a principle of reciprocity, but without any clear sense of who is the active agent in the transaction. Physically, this is a work meant to be displayed in a six by five grid of thirty images, rows A through F, columns 1 through 5. With few exceptions, the individual images show us objects that we can scarcely identify as objects. Some appear to be weird Rube Goldberg contraptions, while some seem to be only graphic configurations of figure and line, light and shadow.

The work, however, is a kind of relentless demonstration of how visual meaning can be produced without the comforts of object constancy, or images that function as markers of temporal intervals. Instead, the array is composed so that it can be read as six lines of five "propositions," each one of which is homologous to a "proposition" on the next line. Thus, we are confronted with a kind of visual acrostic or crossword puzzle, in which there is a graphic cadence observed on each row, stating a "theme" embodied not in a concept but in an affective response; and each column as we read down, plays a "variation" on the previous theme.

It should be noted, for interpretation, that some of the paraphernalia in these photographs does actually have a purpose: it is gear used in pscyhological experiments of several kinds, most notably, experiments with birds, designed to measure or detect their responses to stimuli of various sorts. In one column, for example, the outlines of birds are in fact outlines of various kinds of predators, to which young birds of vulnerable species will instinctively react.

If, in looking at this display, one gets the sense of being a member of a vulnerable species, being experimented upon, it is with good reason. For in this work, Paris employs the principle of the homologue to position these rows of images so that resemblances between one row and those beneath it can be discerned, without requiring any particular thing to be constant or identical.

One may then react to the whole display, much as chicks who have never seen a peregrine falcon will react to a shadow on the ground. What we see, that is, we recognize as a signficant pattern, even if we cannot say what it is. The difference, of course, is that we, unlike baby chicks, have no evolutionary stake in the response—or at least, if we do, it is not so immediately perilous.

What is difficult, then, is how to factor the affect in looking at these abstract images, and the fact of their abstractness. Again, the title offers a valuable clue. If observing modifies the observed, we, as observers, are insinuated into the structure of the array, so that we must look not just at it, but around and through it. The "array" is not just the pictures on a wall or on the page, but is the transaction in which we are both the agent and the object. What we are invited to observe is thus not something given to perception, but something required of it: an act of participatory imagination.

William S. Paris

Prints "A-2, A-3, A-4, A-5" (reading left to right),
from *Observing Modifies the Observed.* 1981
Six rows of five prints
Courtesy of the artist

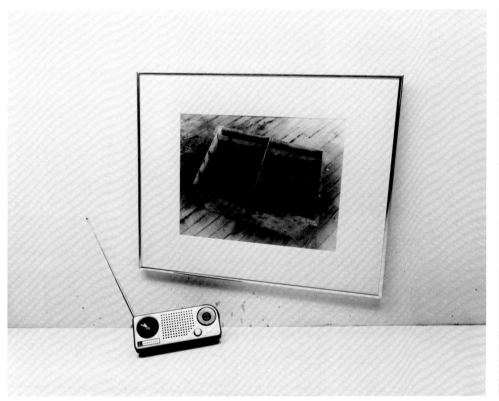

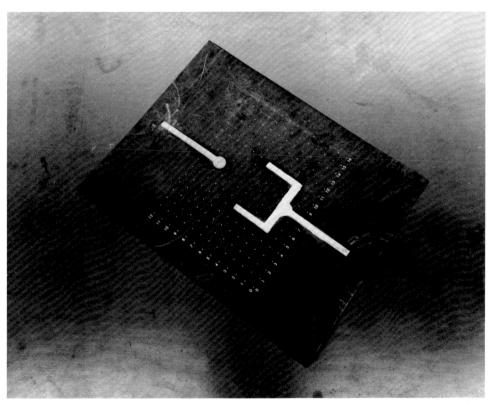

William S. Paris

Rows B, C and D from *Observing
Modifies the Observed.* 1981
Six rows of five prints
Courtesy of the artist

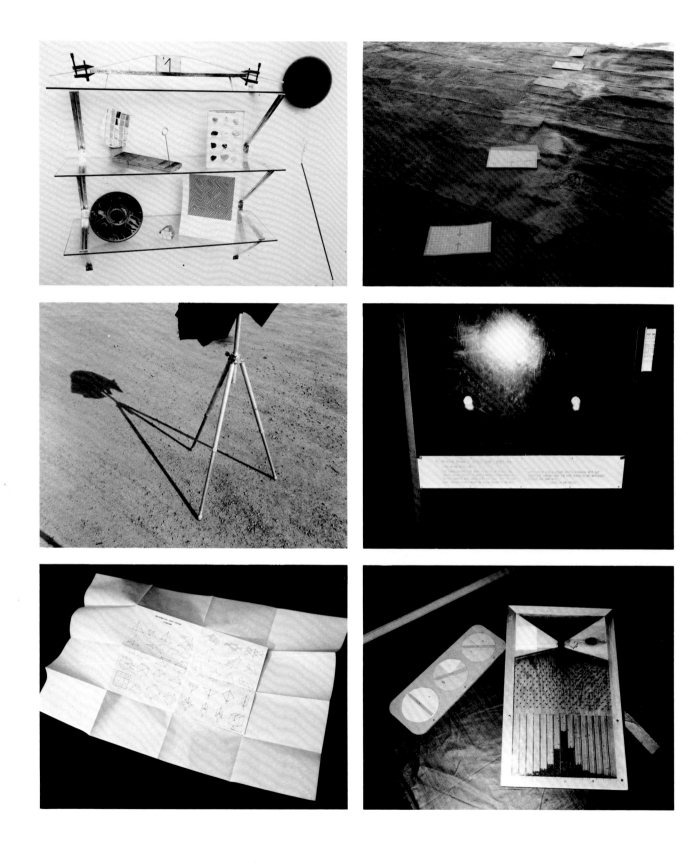

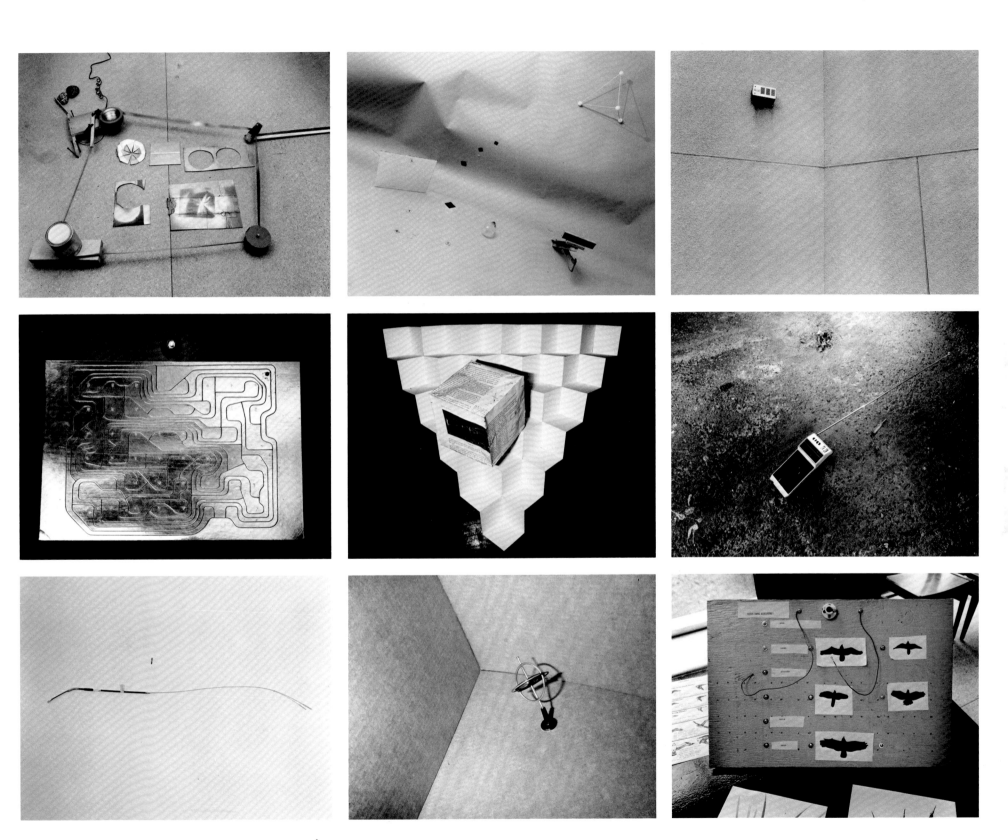

Detail of opposing page.

The single image below is a detail from the opposing page, which is a same size (1:1) reproduction of a portion of Robbert Flick's mosaic Near Live Oak 1, Joshua Tree National Monument, California *(see page 58).*

In the work of Robbert Flick and Joseph Deal, we find perhaps the fullest expressions of the idea network we have followed here. It is immediately striking that Flick employs the format of the grid to exemplify the logic of his own sensitive investigations, while Deal, in *The Fault Zone,* can dispense with it. Yet that is in part, I submit, because both Flick and Deal understand with great visual acuity how pictorial logic produces meaning. On close examination of Flick's prints, for example, it becomes clear that he effects a kind of triangulation in which all three terms can be allowed to vary without disrupting the context.

Thus, the multiple views of *Ocean 2* present individual exposures, bearing a homologous relation to the others, while the whole array is homologous to other Flick landscapes. This is a remarkable achievement. From print to print, one can recover subtle variations of strategy, controlling distance, movement, background, all in the scope of the single integrated display.

The effect resembles, on occasion, Byzantine mosaic, save that the result is neither Byzantine nor mosaic. In *Near Live Oak 1, Joshua Tree National Monument, California,* for example, a limited set of topographical views is presented, in a prodigious orchestration of variations. The result is a single image that has, in the whole, the characteristic look to be found in each of the parts. Here, on the level of particular details, is the embedded employment of the crude syntax of the grid: the order in the parts is replicated in the whole, where identity and substitution create the idea that is the whole picture.

Perhaps even more remarkable, however, is Joseph Deal's *The Fault Zone.* Here, the photographs record something that cannot be seen directly—the geological boundary marked by the San Andreas Fault system. While we may entertain crypto-apocalyptic fantasies of Los Angeles (the "fault zone") slipping off into the sea in the next major earthquake, the fault zone is a conceptual attempt to rationalize space on a scale, and in a set of terms, that can be graphed, but not photographed directly. That is, the geologic fault one can draw on a map; but when one visits particular sites where the fault is said to run, one sees not the fault per se, but landscapes of almost exotic subtlety.

Thus, in this extended sequence of 19 prints, Deal, very much in the context of the idea network shared by other photographers represented in this book, scans a landscape and maps visual relations appearing in it without ever resorting to a crude device. In each print in the sequence, all the material properties of the photographic print are exquisitely turned out, to display an equally exquisite visual intelligence. With great subtlety, these prints create a coherent visual environment: they ARE the "fault zone," and not just a reference to it.

The idea of a fault zone is thereby rendered visible, by depicting the precise (and peculiar) topographic details of 19 places, including the weeds and the wind, the sun and the suburbs, the earthscape and the tracks of the earthmovers.

Considered in juxtaposition, Flick and Deal show remarkable similarities, even as almost every detail of procedure or method differs. In the extended sequence and the array, handled with such integrity, it is perhaps more remarkable that these photographers, even as they are experimenting, show their profound kinship with the historical masters of the medium. Like Jackson and O'Sullivan, but also like Muybridge, Flick and Deal employ the medium as a tool of exploration, with the most satisfying result: their experiments return to affirm the classic traditions of the photographic print.

L. S.

Detail of *Near Live Oak 1, Joshua Tree National Monument, California.* 1981
Print made from 81 negatives in nine rows of nine.
Courtesy of the artist and Tortue Gallery, Santa Monica

Robbert Flick

Near Live Oak 1, Joshua Tree National Monument, California. 1981
Print made from 81 negatives in nine rows of nine
Courtesy of the artist and Tortue Gallery, Santa Monica

Once Flick's entire array is seen, the mosaic gives the illusion of one landscape which is in fact non-existent. On the opposing page however, Joseph Deal's single photograph is actually a component from a larger, invisible landscape, the fault zone.

San Bernardino, California, 1978 (II), from *The
Fault Zone,* 1981
Seattle Art Museum

Robbert Flick

Ocean 2. 1981
Print made from 81 negatives in nine rows of nine
Courtesy of the artist and Tortue Gallery, Santa
Monica

Corn 1. 1980
Print made from 81 negatives
Courtesy of the artist and Tortue Gallery, Santa
Monica

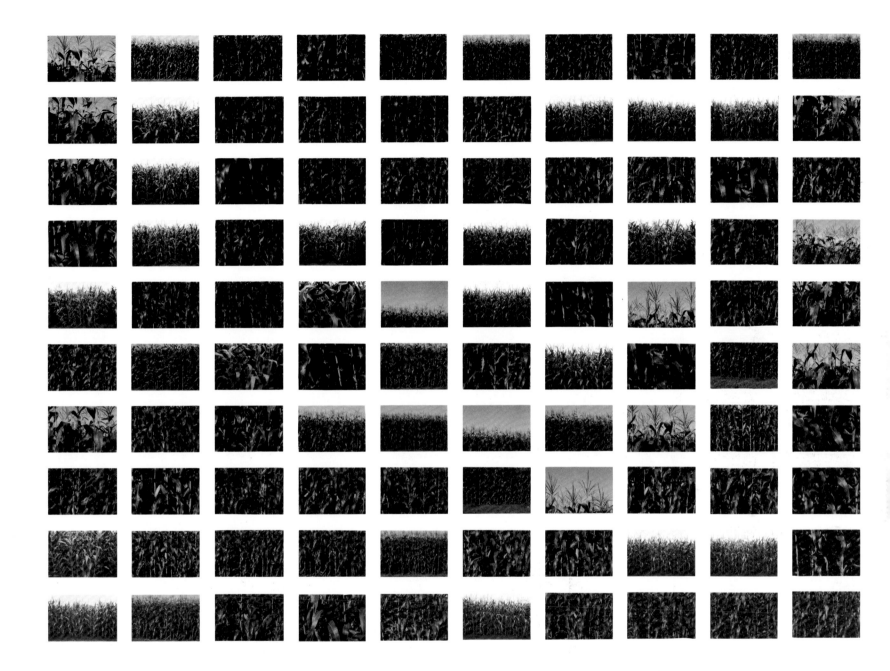

Robbert Flick

Centinella Park, along Florence Boulevard,
looking north, Inglewood, California. 1980
Print made from 81 negatives in nine rows of nine
Courtesy of the artist and Tortue Gallery, Santa
Monica

Joseph Deal

Brea, California, 1979, from *The Fault Zone,* 1981
Seattle Art Museum

below
Soboba Hot Springs, California, 1979 (II), from
The Fault Zone, 1981
Seattle Art Museum

Fontana, California, 1978, from *The Fault Zone,*
1981
Seattle Art Museum

below
Glendale, California, 1979, from *The Fault Zone,*
1981
Seattle Art Museum

Joseph Deal

Colton, California, 1978, from *The Fault Zone,*
1981
Seattle Art Museum

William Henry Jackson

Mountain of the Holy Cross. 1873
United States Geological Survey, Denver

When the Rephotographic Survey Project first
visited the site of Jackson's famous Mountain of
the Holy Cross in 1977, the snowfall had been
unusually light and the accumulation substantially
less than on the comparable date in 1873 when
Jackson had photographed it. When Jackson was
there, the snow-packed cracks in the mountain

formed the awe-inspiring cruciform shape that is
now so familiar to us, but by the seventh decade of
the 20th century, the mountain could only muster a
hesitant apostrophe. The "Mountain of the Holy
Apostrophe" they jokingly called it as they hiked
back down the rugged terrain. Who knows,

MOUNTAIN of the HOLY CROSS, in the GREAT NATIONAL RANGE of COLORADO.

perhaps the mountain was 'saying what it had to say' as articulately on that day as it had been for Jackson more than 100 years earlier.

JoAnn Verburg and Gordon Bushaw
for the Rephotographic Survey Project

Mountain of the Holy Cross, Colorado. 1977
Courtesy of the artists

Mark Klett and Gordon Bushaw
for the Rephotographic Survey Project

Mountain of the Holy Cross, Colorado. 1978
Courtesy of the artists

JoAnn Verburg and Gordon Bushaw
for the Rephotographic Survey Project

Mark Klett and Gordon Bushaw
for the Rephotographic Survey Project

Bernd and Hilla Becher

Joseph Deal

Robbert Flick

Bernd Becher
Born: 1931, Seigen, Germany
Resides: Düsseldorf, Germany
Hilla Becher
Born: 1934, Potsdam, Germany
Resides: Düsseldorf, Germany

Born: 1947, Topeka, Kansas
Resides: Riverside, California

Born: 1939, Amersfoort, Holland
Resides: Inglewood, California

Note on the Checklist

Herein are listed all the works included in the exhibition. The titles of those that are illustrated appear in **boldface**; the page on which they appear is given in parentheses after the title. All "silver prints" are on fiber-base paper unless otherwise noted. Standard sizes for sheets of photographic printing paper, e.g. 8 x 10 and 11 x 14 inches, are given if variation is less than ⅛ inch. Prints are printed by the artist unless otherwise stated.

All works consist of separately mounted silver prints, each measuring 20 x 16 in (50.8 x 40.6 cm) unless otherwise noted. Courtesy of the artists and Sonnabend Gallery, New York, unless otherwise noted.

Cooling Towers. 1978 **(pp.46, 47)**
16 prints, 15¹⁵/₁₆ x 12⅛ in (40.5 x 30.8 cm) each, displayed in two rows of eight
Collection of Bing Wright

Winding Towers. 1982 **(p.17)**
15 prints, displayed in three rows of five

Blast Furnace Heads. 1982 **(p. 48)**
15 prints, displayed in three rows of five

All photographs are gold-toned silver prints, measuring 13¾ x 13¾ in (34.9 x 34.9 cm). Collection of Seattle Art Museum, purchased with funds from Pacific Northwest Bell, the Photography Council, the Polaroid Foundation, Mark Abrahamson, and the National Endowment for the Arts.

The Fault Zone. 1981

Colton, California, 1978. **(p. 64)**

Indio, California, 1978.

Fontana, California, 1978. **(p. 63)**

San Bernardino, California, 1978 (I). **(p. 19)**

San Bernardino, California, 1978 (II). **(p. 59)**

Santa Barbara, California, 1978.

Baldwin Hills, California, 1979.

Brea, California, 1979. **(p. 63)**

Glendale, California, 1979. **(p. 63)**

Hemet, California, 1979.

Inglewood, California, 1979.

Monrovia, California, 1979.

Near Beaumont, California, 1979.

Newport Beach, California, 1979.

Palm Springs, California, 1979.

San Fernando, California, 1979. **(pp. 10, 65)**

Soboba Hot Springs, California, 1979 (I).

Soboba Hot Springs, California, 1979 (II). **(p. 63)**

Chatsworth, California, 1980.

All photographs are silver prints made using 81 negatives, measuring 20 x 24 in (50.8 x 61 cm) unless noted otherwise. Courtesy of the artist and Tortue Gallery, Santa Monica.

Sequential Views

Ocean 1. 1980
16 x 20 in (40.6 x 50.8 cm)

Ocean Park, California, along Ocean Park Blvd., looking west. 1980
16 x 20 in (40.6 x 50.8 cm)

Santa Monica Beach, looking east, Santa Monica, California. 1980
16 x 20 in (40.6 x 50.8 cm)

Manhattan Beach, looking north, from Marine. 1980

Corn 1. 1980 **(p. 61)**
16 x 20 in (40.6 x 50.8 cm)

Centinella Park, along Florence Blvd., looking north, Inglewood, California. 1980 **(p. 62)**

Manhattan Beach, looking west, from Vista. 1980

F.A.A., along Imperial Blvd., looking north. 1980
16 x 20 in (40.6 x 50.8 cm)

Venice Beach, California, Labor Day Weekend. 1980
16 x 20 in (40.6 x 50.8 cm)

Ocean 2. 1981 **(pp. 49, 60)**

Chicago Forest Preserve, Illinois. 1981

Parking Structure #2, Inglewood, California. 1981

Near Live Oak 1, Joshua Tree National Monument, California. 1981 **(pp. 56, 57, 58)**

N.E. of Backus Road, Kern County, California. 1981

Ocean 3, (dawn). 1982

Catalina 1 (Parsons Landing), California. 1982

"Bay View," Parsons Landing, California. 1982

Solstice Canyon #8. 1982 **(p. 18)**

Surf 1. 1982

At Vasquez Rocks 1, L.A. County Park, California. 1982

Near Live Oak 2, Joshua Tree National Monument, California. 1982

Marion Faller and Hollis Frampton   **Bill Ganzel**

Marion Faller
Born: 1941, Wallington, New Jersey
Resides: Buffalo, New York
Hollis Frampton
Born: 1936, Wooster, Ohio
Resides: Buffalo, New York

Born: 1949, Lincoln, Nebraska
Resides: Lincoln, Nebraska

All photographs are silver prints made using 12 negatives and measure 11 x 14 in (28 x 35.6 cm). Courtesy of the artists and Visual Studies Workshop Gallery, Rochester.

"Sixteen Studies from
Vegetable Locomotion." **1975**

14. *Gourds vanishing (var. "Mixed*
Ornamental"). **(p. 45)**

33. *Zucchini squash encountering sawhorse*
(var. "Dread").

39. *Sunflower reclining (var. "Mammoth*
Russian"). **(p. 7)**

121. *Scallop squash revolving (var. "Patty Pan").*

260. *Savoy cabbage flying (var. "Chieftain").*

357. *Summer squash undergoing surgery*
(var. "Yellow Straightneck").

481. *Mature radishes bathing (var. "Black*
Spanish").

482. *Pumpkin emptying (var. "Cinderella").*

484. *Winter squash vacillating (var. "True*
Hubbard").

519. *Tomatoes descending a ramp (var. "Roma").*

537. *Watermelon falling (var. "New Hampshire*
Midget").

601. *Sweet corn disrobing (var. "Early Sunglow").*

605. *Dill bundling (var. "Rural Splendor").*

668. *Beets assembling (var. "Detroit Dark Red").*

709. *Carrot ejaculating (var. "Chantenay").*

782. *Apple advancing (var. "Northern*
Spy"). **(p. 43)**

All works consist of an FSA and a Ganzel photograph, each measuring 11 x 14 in (27.9 x 35.6 cm), mounted together with their captions and often with oral history accounts from people in the photographs (see pages 32-33 for example). All are silver prints unless noted otherwise; Mr. Ganzel has made copy photographs of FSA images for display. FSA images courtesy of the Library of Congress, Washington, D.C.; Ganzel images courtesy of the artist.

Dorothea Lange
Migrant Mother [*Florence Thompson with her*
daughters: Norma, in her arms; Katherine, left;
and Ruby]. **(p. 25)**
Nipomo, California
March 1936
Bill Ganzel
Florence Thompson and her daughters Norma
Rydlewski (in front), Katherine McIntosh, and
Ruby Sprague, at Norma's house. **(p. 25)**
Modesto, California
June 1979

Arthur Rothstein
Fleeing a dust storm [*from left, Milton, Arthur*
and Darrel Coble]. **(p. 12)**
Cimarron County, Oklahoma
April 1936
Bill Ganzel
Darrel Coble in his home. On the wall is a
painting by a local woman copied from Rothstein's
photograph. In 1977, Darrel lived about 12 miles
from where the photograph was taken. Arthur, his
father, and Milton, his older brother, had died, and
Darrel died in 1980. **(p. 13)**
Cimarron County, Oklahoma
September 1977

Arthur Rothsten
Wife of a farmsteader [*Mrs. Harvey Taft*].
(p. 36)
Falls City Farmstead, Nebraska
May 1936
Bill Ganzel
Arthur Rothstein in the "cave" on Harvey Taft's
farm. Harvey was one of the original members of
the FSA-sponsored cooperative farmstead and
bought most of the land and buildings when the
program ended in the early forties. **(p. 37)**
North of Falls City, Nebraska
September 1979

Arthur Rothstein
Vernon Evans [*and*] *his family of Lemmon, South*
Dakota, on Highway #10, left the grasshopper-
ridden and drought stricken area for a new start in
Oregon or Washington. They expect to arrive at
Yakima, Washington, in time for hop-picking. They
live in a tent and make about 200 miles a day in a
Model-T Ford. **(p. 32)**
Missoula (vicinity), Montana
July [18,] 1936
Bill Ganzel
Vernon Evans on the farm his father homesteaded
and to which Vernon returned after nine years in
Oregon. **(p. 33)**
Lemmon, South Dakota
July 18, 1977

Dorothea Lange
Former Texas tenant farmers displaced by power
farming [*from left: O. B. Welch, Cephus*
Montgomery, Raymond Turpen, Vernon Scott,
D. W. Welch, and Walter Ballard]. *All displaced*
tenant farmers, the oldest 33. All on WPA. They
support an average of four persons each on
$22.80 a month. "I can count 23 farmers in the
west half of this county that have had to leave the
farms to give three men more land" (from Lange
and Taylor, American Exodus).
Hardeman County, Texas
May 1937
Bill Ganzel
Raymond Turpen and Walter Ballard.
Hardeman County, near Goodlett, Texas
July 1979

Russell Lee
William Huravitch, farmer.
Williams County, North Dakota
September 1937
Bill Ganzel
William Huravitch in front of his old house.
Williams County, North Dakota
November 1979

Russell Lee
Family of Floyd Peacher in the living room of their
farm house.
Williston (vicinity), North Dakota
September 1937
Bill Ganzel
Mrs. Clara Melland, who was married to Floyd
Peacher during the thirties, with photographs of
some of her 12 children.
Williston, North Dakota
November 1979

Russell Lee
Daughter of Joe Kramer [*Florence*] *whose dwarfed*
arm is probably due to infantile paralysis.
Williston (vicinity), North Dakota
October 1937
Bill Ganzel
Florence Kramer. Her left arm was damaged by
polio at the age of two and she now walks with a
cane. She has never been able to work and has
lived for 11 years in a small room at the S&L Hotel.
Meals are served in a communal dining room, and
once a week a maid cleans the room.
Williston, North Dakota
November 1979

Dorothea Lange
Woman of the high plains [*Nettie Featherston*].
"If you die, you're dead – that's all."
Texas Panhandle, Childress [vicinity]
June 1938
Bill Ganzel
Nettie Featherson in the four-room house she
shares with her son.
Lubbock, Texas
August 1979

John Vachon
Barn on a large farm, Red River Valley.
Cass County, North Dakota
November 1938
Bill Ganzel
Hog barn and chicken on the Barker farm.
Near Gardner, Red River Valley, Cass County,
North Dakota
July 1977
Cibachrome print

Dorothea Lange
County courthouse just before primary election.
Waco, Texas
1938
Bill Ganzel
Joe Alexander with his 1938 campaign poster, in
front of the McLennan County Courthouse,
during election week.
Waco, Texas
November 1978

John Vachon
U.S. Highway #281.
Aberdeen (vicinity), South Dakota
February 1942
Bill Ganzel
Recruiting poster, U.S. Highway #30.
Shelton (vicinity), Nebraska
April 1975

Frank Gohlke

Born: 1942, Wichita Falls, Texas
Resides: Minneapolis, Minnesota

All works consist of two silver prints, measuring
16 x 20 in (40.6 x 50.8 cm), displayed vertically.
Courtesy of the artist.

Aftermath: The Wichita Falls Tornado. 1982

*Southmoor Manor Apartments, looking north,
April 14, 1979.*
*Southmoor Manor Apartments, looking north,
June 1980.*

*Southmoor Manor Apartments, looking west,
April 14, 1979.*
*Southmoor Manor Apartments, looking west,
June 1980.*

*Southmoor Manor Apartments, looking north,
April 14, 1979.*
*Southmoor Manor Apartments, looking north,
June 1980.*

*Southmoor Manor Apartments, looking south,
April 14, 1979.*
*Southmoor Manor Apartments, looking south,
June 1980.*

*1500 Block Hursh Avenue, looking west,
April 14, 1979.*
*1500 Block Hursh Avenue, looking west,
June 1980.*

*Alley between Aldrich and Christine Avenues, on
Southmoor Lane,looking east, April 14, 1979.*
*Alley between Aldrich and Christine Avenues, on
Southmoor Lane, looking east, June 1980.*
**1600 Block Aldrich Avenue, looking east,
April 14, 1979.   (p. 31)**
**1600 Block Aldrich Avenue, looking east,
June 1980.   (p. 31)**

*Southmoor Lane, looking southwest toward Lake
Park Drive, April 14, 1979.*
*Southmoor Lane, looking southwest toward Lake
Park Drive, June 1980.*

Sikes Senter Mall, looking northeast, April 14, 1979.
*Sikes Senter Mall, looking northeast,
June 1980.*

**Maplewood Avenue, near Sikes Senter Mall,
looking northeast, April 14, 1979.   (p. 34)**
**Maplewood Avenue, near Sikes Senter Mall,
looking northeast, June 1980.   (p. 35)**

4053 McNeil, looking north, April 14, 1979.
4053 McNeil, looking north, June 1980.
*Willow Creek Apartments, 4835 Barnett Road,
looking northeast, April 14, 1979.*
*Willow Creek Apartments, 4835 Barnett Road,
looking northeast, June 1980.*
*View of Faith Village from Kiwanis Park, looking
east, April 14, 1979.*
*View of Faith Village from Kiwanis Park, looking
east, June 1980.*
**View of Faith Village from Kiwanis Park, looking
east, April 15, 1979.   (p. 36)**
**View of Faith Village from Kiwanis Park, looking
east, June 1980.   (p. 37)**
*Northwest corner of Fairway and Southwest
Parkway, April 15, 1979.*
*Northwest corner of Fairway and Southwest
Parkway, June 1980.*
*Backyard of 4611 Belmont, looking north,
April 15, 1979.*
*Backyard of 4611 Belmont, looking north,
June 1980.*
4611 Belmont, looking west, April 15, 1979.
4611 Belmont, looking west, June 1980.
**4673 Woodlawn, looking west,
April 15, 1979.   (p. 30)**
**4673 Woodlawn, looking west,
June 1980.   (p. 30)**
4679 University, looking west, April 15, 1979.
4679 University, looking west, June 1980.
**Southwest Parkway near Fairway, looking west,
April 15, 1979.   (p. 14)**
**Southwest Parkway near Fairway, looking west,
June 1980.   (p. 15)**

Gary Metz

Born: 1941, Detroit, Michigan
Resides: New York City

All photographs are silver prints, measuring
14 x 11 in (35.6 x 27.9 cm). Courtesy of the artist.

***Hair Piece ("Every Force Has Its Form"–Shaker
Saying).   (pp. 16, 50, 51)***
30 prints from this continuing, open-ended
series, all dating from the years 1977-79,
were displayed.

Eadweard Muybridge

Born: 1830, Kingston-on-Thames
Died: 1904, Kingston-on-Thames

All works consist of multiple negatives printed
on a single sheet. Unless noted otherwise,
works are from the Stanford Family Collection,
Stanford University Museum of Art.

Abe Edgington Trotting, from *The Horse in
Motion,* published by Morse, 1879   **(pp. 6, 42)**
Albumen print made from 12 negatives in three
rows of three
5¼ x 8½ in (13.3 x 21.6 cm)
Collection of R. Joseph and Elaine R. Monsen

Indian Elephant Ambling, Plate 733, *Animal
Locomotion,* University of Pennsylvania,
1887   **(p. 44)**
Collotype plate made from 24 negatives printed
in four rows of six
8¹/₁₆ x 14⅞ in (20.7 x 37.1 cm)

Walking on Hands and Feet, Plate 183, *Animal
Locomotion,* University of Pennsylvania, 1887
Collotype plate made from 12 negatives in two
rows of six
6⅜ x 17¾ in (16.1 x 45.1 cm)

Lifting a Log on Shoulder, Plate 383, *Animal
Locomotion,* University of Pennsylvania, 1887
Collotype plate made from 24 negatives in
three rows of four
7⅜ x 14⅞ in (18.7 x 37.1 cm)

Esther Parada

William S. Paris

Rephotographic Survey Project

Born: 1938, Grand Rapids, Michigan
Resides: Skokie, Illinois

Born: 1954, Rochester, New York
Resides: Rochester, New York

Gordon Bushaw
Born: 1947, Colfax, Washington
Resides: Poulsbo, Washington

Rick Dingus
Born: 1951, Appleton City, Wisconsin
Resides: Lubbock, Texas

Mark Klett
Born: 1952, Albany, New York
Resides: Tucson, Arizona

Ellen Manchester
Born: 1945, Hanover, New Hampshire
Resides: San Francisco, California

JoAnn Verburg
Born: 1950, Summit, New Jersey
Resides: Minneapolis, Minnesota

All works are composites of 25 6 x 6 in (15.2 x 15.2 cm) silver prints mounted contiguously in five rows of five each; overall dimensions are 30 x 30 in (76.2 x 76.2 cm). Courtesy of the artist.

Memory Warp series

Memory Warp I. 1980

Memory Warp II. 1980   (p. 39)

Memory Warp III. 1980   (p. 40)

All photographs are silver prints, each measuring 14 x 11 in (35.6 x 27.9 cm). Courtesy of the artist.

***Observing Modifies the Observed.* 1981 (pp. 52, 53, 54, 55)**
Six rows of five prints

For exhibition, the RSP has made copy prints of the original United States Geological Survey photographs—the originals of which were albumen prints or were published as lithographs or some other conversion—that are then matched with rephotographs of the same size: each is an 8 x 10 in (20.3 x 27.9 cm) silver print. Such pairs formed the majority of those exhibited, with the exception of five original William H. Jackson prints and same-size rephotographs, which are listed separately below, and three 8 x 10 inch silver print pairs supplemented with color versions of the rephotograph. The U.S.G.S., Denver, was the source of all original Survey material unless noted otherwise. All rephotographs are courtesy of the RSP.

William H. Jackson
Colorado City, Cheyene Mountain. 1873
JoAnn Verburg for the RSP *Garden of the Gods, Colorado, Panorama (left).* 1977

William H. Jackson
Garden of the Gods, Pikes Peak. 1873
JoAnn Verburg for the RSP
Garden of the Gods, Colorado, Panorama (right). 1977

William H. Jackson
Castle Rock, Boulder Cañon. 1873
JoAnn Verburg for the RSP
Castle Rock, Boulder Canyon, Colorado. 1977

William H. Jackson
Boulder Cañon near Castle Rock. 1873
JoAnn Verburg for the RSP
Boulder Canyon, Colorado. 1977

William H. Jackson
Grotto Geyser. c 1883
Mark Klett and Gordon Bushaw for the RSP
Grotto Geyser, Yellowstone National Park, Wyoming. 1978

William H. Jackson
Grand Cañon of the Yellowstone. 1872
Museum of New Mexico
Mark Klett and Gordon Bushaw for the RSP
Grand Canyon of the Yellowstone, Yellowstone National Park, Wyoming. 1978

William H. Jackson
Hot Springs and the Castle Geyser. 1872
Yellowstone National Park
Mark Klett and Gordon Bushaw for the RSP
Crested Hot Springs and Castle Geyser, Yellowstone National Park, Wyoming. 1978

William H. Jackson
Crater of the Castle Geyser. c 1872
Mark Klett and Gordon Bushaw for the RSP
Crater of the Castle Geyser, Yellowstone National Park, Wyoming. 1978

Timothy H. O'Sullivan
Provo Cañon Cliffs, 2,000 ft. limestones, Utah Territory, Wahsatch Mountain. c 1869
Rick Dingus for the RSP
Bridal Veil Falls, Provo Canyon, Utah. 1978

Timothy H. O'Sullivan
Untitled. c 1869
Rick Dingus for the RSP
Picnic Ground, Storm Mountain, Big Cottonwood Canyon, Utah. 1978

Timothy H. O'Sullivan
Untitled. c 1869
Rick Dingus for the RSP
Edge of Storm Mountain Reservoir, Big Cottonwood Canyon, Utah. 1978

A. J. Russell
Hanging Rock Foot of Echo Cañon. 1868
Yale University
Rick Dingus for the RSP
Hanging Rock Foot of Echo Canyon. 1978

Timothy H. O'Sullivan
Conglomerate Column, Weber Valley, (Lithograph) Plate XIII, Descriptive Geology, Vol. II, by Hague and Emmons. 1869
Rick Dingus for the RSP
The Drumstick, Weber Valley, Utah. 1978

Timothy H. O'Sullivan
Tertiary Conglomerates, Weber Valley, Utah. 1869
Rick Dingus for the RSP
Witches Rocks, Weber Valley, Utah. 1978

William H. Jackson
Pulpit Rock at the Mouth of the Canyon. 1869
Rick Dingus for the RSP
Site of Pulpit Rock, Echo Canyon, Utah. 1978

Timothy H. O'Sullivan
Devil's Slide Weber Cañon, Utah, (Lithograph) Plate XII from Systems Geology, Vol. II, by King. 1869
Rick Dingus for the RSP
Devil's Slide, Weber Canyon, Utah. 1978

William H. Jackson
Silverton, Colorado. c 1880
Colorado Historical Society
Gordon Bushaw for the RSP
Silverton, Colorado, left half. 1978

William H. Jackson
Silverton, Colorado. c 1880
Colorado Historical Society
Gordon Bushaw for the RSP
Silverton, Colorado, right half. 1978

Timothy H. O'Sullivan
*Green River Cañon, Upper Cañon, Great Bend,
Uinta Mountains, The Horseshoe and Green River
Below the Bend from Flaming Gorge Ridge.*
c 1872
Mark Klett for the RSP
*Flaming Gorge Reservoir from Above the Site of
the Great Bend, Wyoming.* 1978

Timothy H. O'Sullivan
Tertiary Bluffs near Green River City, Wyoming.
c 1872
Mark Klett for the RSP
*Teapot Rock and the Sugarbowl, Green River,
Wyoming.* 1978
Type C color rephotograph also displayed.

Timothy H. O'Sullivan
Tertiary Bluffs near Green River Station. c 1872
Mark Klett for the RSP
The Giant's Thumb," near Green River, Wyoming.
1978

William H. Jackson
A Study Among the Rocks of Echo Canyon. 1869
Gordon Bushaw for the RSP
Rocks, Echo Canyon, Utah. 1978

Timothy H. O'Sullivan
*Tertiary Columns, Green River City, Wyoming
(Lithograph) Plate VI, Descriptive Geology, Vol. II,
by Hague and Emmons.* c 1872
Mark Klett for the RSP
Sugar Bowl and Teapot, Green River, Wyoming.
1978

Timothy H. O'Sullivan
Spanish Inscriptions, Inscription Rock. 1873
(p. 20)
Rick Dingus for the RSP
Inscription #20 on the walking tour, Inscription
Rock, New Mexico. 1978   (p. 20)

Timothy H. O'Sullivan
*Cañon de Chelle, Walls of the Grand Cañon about
1,200 feet in height.* 1873
Collection of Van Deren Coke
Mark Klett for the RSP
*Monument Rock, Canyon de Chelly National
Monument, Arizona.* 1978

J. K. Hillers
Ancient Ruins, Cañon de Chelly. n.d.
Collection of Van Deren Coke
Mark Klett for the RSP
*Mummy Cave Ruins, Canyon del Muerte, Canyon
de Chelly National Monument, Arizona.* 1978

William H. Jackson
Liberty Cap. 1872
Mark Klett for the RSP
Liberty Cap, Yellowstone National Park, Wyoming.
1978

Timothy H. O'Sullivan
Virginia City, Comstock Mines. 1868
Museum of New Mexico
Mark Klett for the RSP
*Strip Mines at the site of Comstock Mines,
Virginia City, Nevada.* 1979
Type C color rephotograph also displayed.

Timothy H. O'Sullivan
Quartz Mill near Virginia City. 1868   (p. 28)
Mark Klett for the RSP
Site of the Gould and Curry Mine, Virginia City,
Nevada. 1979   (p. 29)

Timothy H. O'Sullivan
Green River Buttes, Green River, Wyoming.
c 1872   (p. 28)
Mark Klett and Gordon Bushaw for the RSP
Castle Rock, Green River, Wyoming. 1979
(p. 29)
Type C color rephotograph also displayed.

Timothy H. O'Sullivan
Rock Formations, Pyramid Lake, Nevada. 1867
Massachusetts Institute of Technology
Mark Klett for the RSP
Pyramid Isle, Pyramid Lake, Nevada. 1979

In the following five cases, original William H.
Jackson photographs were paired with same-size
rephotographs, each measuring 9 x 13 in
(23 x 33 cm) unless otherwise noted.

William H. Jackson
*Eroded Sandstones, Monument Park, Colorado
(Eroded Sandstones, Monument Park No. 72).*
1873
Albumen print
12½ x 10 in (31.7 x 25.3 cm)
International Museum of Photography at
George Eastman House
JoAnn Verburg for the RSP
*Eroded Sandstones, Woodman Road, Colorado
Springs, Colorado.* 1977
Silver print
12½ x 10 in (31.7 x 25.3 cm)

William H. Jackson
**Cathedral Spires, Garden of the Gods, Colorado
(Montezuma's Cathedral, Garden of the Gods).
1873   (p. 11)**
Albumen print
8 x 12⅞ in (20.5 x 32.8 cm)
International Museum of Photography at
George Eastman House
Mark Klett and JoAnn Verburg for the RSP
**Faulted Rocks, Garden of the Gods, Colorado.
1977   (p. 11)**
Silver print
8 x 12⅞ in (20.5 x 32.8 cm)

William H. Jackson
Mountain of the Holy Cross. 1873   (p. 66)
Albumen print
International Museum of Photography at
George Eastman House
JoAnn Verburg and Gordon Bushaw
for the RSP
Mountain of the Holy Cross, Colorado. 1977
(p. 67)
Silver print
Mark Klett and Gordon Bushaw for the RSP
Mountain of the Holy Cross, Colorado. 1978
(p. 67)
Silver print

William H. Jackson
*Moraines on Clear Creek, Valley of the Arkansas,
Colorado.* 1873
Albumen print
International Museum of Photography at
George Eastman House
Mark Klett and JoAnn Verburg for the RSP
Clear Creek Reservoir, Colorado. 1977
Silver print

William H. Jackson
**Snow Mass Mountain and Elk Lake, Elk
Mountains (White House Mountain, Elk Lake).
1873   (p. 22)**
Albumen print
International Museum of Photography at
George Eastman House
Mark Klett and JoAnn Verburg for the RSP
**Snow Mass Mountain, Geneva Lake, Colorado.
1977   (p. 22)**
Silver print

Eve Sonneman

Born: 1946, Chicago, Illinois
Resides: New York City

All works consist of 2 Cibachrome color prints
mounted horizontally. Each print measures 8 x 10 in
(20.3 x 25.4 cm). Editions are limited to 10. Unless
otherwise noted, works are courtesy of the artist
and Castelli Graphics, New York.

Western Views: Motel, Silver City. 1975

The Culture Park, Izmir, Turkey. 1977

*Two Grapepickers Pausing for Water, Samos,
Greece.* 1977

The Instant and the Moment, Greece. 1977

A Man and his Donkey, Samos, Greece. 1977

Boat in the Bush, Española, New Mexico. 1978

Shadows, Santa Fe, New Mexico. 1978

Grapes, New York. 1979
Washington Art Consortium Collection

Memory, New York. 1979   (p. 38)

Flowers, Bordeaux. 1980

Malpensa to Milan. 1980

Newspaper, New York. 1980   (p. 41)